Information-Driven Business

INFORMATION-DRIVEN BUSINESS

How to Manage Data and Information for Maximum Advantage

ROBERT HILLARD

WILEY

John Wiley & Sons, Inc.

Published by John Wiley & Sons, Inc., Hoboken, New Jersey.
Published simultaneously in Canada.

For general information on our other products and services or for technical support, please
contact our Customer Care Department within the United States at (800) 762-2974,
outside the United States at (317) 572-3993 or fax (317) 572-4002.

Wiley also publishes its books in a variety of electronic formats. Some content that
appears in print may not be available in electronic books. For more information about
Wiley products, visit our Web site at www.wiley.com.

Library of Congress Cataloging-in-Publication Data

Hillard, Robert, 1968–
    Information-driven business : how to manage data and information for maximum
advantage / Robert Hillard.
       p. cm.
    Includes bibliographical references and index.
    ISBN 978-0-470-62577-4 (cloth); ISBN 978-0-470-64943-5 (ebk);
ISBN 978-0-470-64945-9 (ebk); ISBN 978-0-470-64946-6 (ebk)
    1. Technological innovations—Management.   2. Information technology—
Management.   3. Management information systems.   4. Industrial management.
I. Title.
    HD45.H45 2010
    658.4′038–dc22

                2010007798

Printed in the United States of America.

10 9 8 7 6 5 4 3 2 1

To A, I, and M with love.

Contents

Preface

This book is aimed at anyone who is in any way responsible for information. Executives, managers, and technical staff all need to understand how to manage this most valuable resource.

I wrote this book based on the observation that the concept of information overload is permeating every business that I deal with. At the same time, the global economy is moving from products to services that are described almost entirely electronically. Even those businesses that are traditionally associated with making things are less concerned with the management of the manufacturing process (which is largely outsourced) than they are with the management of their intellectual property. Increasingly, information doesn't provide a window on the business. *It is the business.*

It's a simple equation. Intellectual property is tied up in the data on computers. If it is the subject of focused management, then greater value is extracted from that data. If the intellectual property is a significant proportion of the value of the business, then such a focused effort will have a dramatic effect on the value of the business as a whole. Such an effort will also make the organization much more enjoyable to work in with less time lost searching for information that should be readily available and less time sifting through irrelevant data that should never have hit the e-mail inbox.

As business has become more complex, techniques are appearing almost every day that seek to simplify the task of managing a large, multifaceted organization. Their quest is similar to a physicist looking for the single unifying equation that will define the universe. Any approach that recommends focusing on one part of the business must use a limited set of measures that aggregate complex data from across the enterprise. In providing a simple answer, detail and differentiation must be lost.

A simple set of metrics by itself is no longer enough to sum up the millions or billions of moving parts that define the enterprise. Perhaps, then, it is time to gain a better understanding of the role of information in business.

While large quantities of information have been with us for as long as humans have gathered in groups, it has taken on a whole new dynamic form. The quantity of data has grown dramatically since the cost of computer storage dropped as it did at the end of the twentieth century. The growth has taken business management by surprise and the techniques that we use have not been able to keep up.

With little differentiation in the bricks-and-mortar assets, business needs to enhance its service and differentiate using the informational resources at its disposal. The winners tailor their product to the needs of their markets. Successful leaders have a deep insight into the running of their business. Such an insight can come only from accurate information.

In almost every organization, one or more executives have been assigned accountability for information governance, quality, or records. Similarly, technologists are being asked to make sense of the mountains of data that exist in databases, file systems, and other repositories. This is a book about becoming an information-centric business and achieving significant benefits as a result.

Over many years, I have had the opportunity to work with hundreds of organizations in the private and government sectors. The issues that they face handling business information have a common theme of complexity. Questions that should be simple to answer take too long, reconciliations that should be exact aren't, privacy that should be perfect isn't, and security that should be tight is porous.

Treating information as something that needs to be managed in its own right allows a profession of information managers to develop a common approach to information management. Without common techniques, many organizations have been ad hoc in their approach. The most successful, though, have borrowed approaches from other disciplines and been part of the evolution of a form of professional consensus.

For that reason, I have been pleased over a number of years to be part of the leadership of the MIKE2.0 initiative. MIKE2.0 (Method for the Implementation of a Knowledge Enterprise) is an open collaboration of information management professionals from a variety of organizations seeking to develop a common approach. The content is entirely free under the Creative Commons licensing model. MIKE2.0 can be found at www.openmethodology.org.

I have applied the techniques in this book in some of the world's largest companies and government departments. They have also been effectively adopted in midsized and even small businesses. As a field grows in sophistication, so the knowledge needed by practitioners also increases. This book provides sufficient detail to allow anyone who deals with information to identify the right approach to apply without trying to be a step-by-step guide. Armed with the knowledge within these pages, the reader can then adopt comprehensive methodologies like MIKE2.0 to develop detailed project plans or establish programs of work.

Each chapter introduces a concept and in many cases provides both strategic and tactical advice. The strategic advice will help shape the future enterprise. The tactical advice will help solve immediate challenges. The reader should be left with the overwhelming message that information management is not the responsibility of the information technology department, nor is it able to be governed by any one line of business. Information is an asset with a very real economic value. It is the responsibility of everyone who in any way creates, handles, stores, or exploits this asset to ensure that they achieve the greatest possible value for the enterprise as a whole.

This is not the final book that will be written on this subject. The discipline will continue to develop as we all find better and more effective ways to run organizations to better create, handle, and exploit information. There is no single answer to the question on how you should manage your information resources, so apart from the MIKE2.0 site, I also encourage readers of this book to check in at www.infodrivenbusiness.com where additional references and comments will be posted.

Acknowledgments

Many people have helped to review draft manuscripts, supported the process of getting it published, and constantly challenged me to think deeply about all aspects of information and data management. I'd like to specifically thank, in no particular order, Robin Hillard, Michelle Pearce, Professor David Arnott, Sean McClowry, Professor Graeme Shanks, Dr. Gregory Hill, Frank Farrall, Gerhard Vorster, Giam Swiegers, Brian Romer, and Michael Tarlinton.

Information-Driven Business

Chapter 1

Understanding the Information Economy

Managing information has become as important to the enterprise as managing financial information has been to the accounting functions of a business. Information now pervades every aspect of an organization, including reporting, marketing, product development, and resource allocation. In the last twenty years, business reports to management and investors have become much more dependent on information derived from nonfinancial sources than ever before.

In fact, as the economy increasingly depends on information, the old assumptions about what is important have changed. The value that business saw in scale due to shared functions and infrastructure have been turned on their head by business process outsourcing (BPO), which is the outsourcing of a business function that might previously have been done within the organization. Examples include the processing of invoices, payroll, or even customer contact through call centers.

BPO is only possible because of advances in the storage, communication, and description of complex information at a cost that is much lower than imaginable even twenty years ago. At the same time, the value that business might previously have seen in owning infrastructure (such as manufacturing plants) has been overtaken by the value of the knowledge of the manufacturing process.

Everywhere we look, we see examples of how the management and exchange of intangible information has become more important than the trade in physical resources. An information economy has been created describing the exchange of information among organizations and between individuals and departments within a single organization.

To extract the greatest possible value from the concept of the information economy, it is worth looking at its origins.

> We should be investing in the new electronic superhighways—satellite and telecommunications technology that is the nerve centre of a new Information Economy— doing for the next century what roads and railways have done for this one.
>
> **—Tony Blair, Labour Party Conference, 1994**

Blair, like most politicians, saw services trading in information as being driven by the Internet and its supporting communications infrastructure. By 1990, however, the networking technologies that drove the Internet were already well established and mature. So why wasn't the economy already online?

1

DID THE INTERNET CREATE
THE INFORMATION ECONOMY?

The concept of electronic or information superhighways appeared as early as the 1970s. Artist Nam June Paik, who is well known for his electronic and video work, appears to be the first person to have used *information superhighway* as a term, in 1974. Certainly, by the 1980s, there are many references to the term. *Newsweek* carried an article on January 3, 1983, which uses the term with reference to networks being built to connect northeastern cities such as New York, Washington, DC, and Boston. Al Gore (Vice President of the United States from 1992 to 2000) and Bill Gates (cofounder of Microsoft) did much to popularize the term in the 1990s.

> The United States could benefit greatly—in research, in education, in economic development, and in scores of other areas—by efficiently processing and dealing with information that is available but unused. What we need is a nationwide network of information superhighways, linking scientists, business people, educators, and students by fiber-optic cable.
>
> **—Al Gore, "Information Superhighways: The Next Information Revolution,"**
> ***The Futurist*, 1991**

> Now that computing is astoundingly inexpensive and computers inhabit every part of our lives, we stand at the brink of another revolution. This one will involve unprecedentedly inexpensive communications. All the computers will join together to communicate with us and for us. Interconnected globally, they'll form a large interactive network, which is sometimes called the information superhighway.
>
> **—Bill Gates, *The Road Ahead*, 1995**

The consistent theme of speeches and commentary from the era is that the Internet combined with ubiquitous connectivity would drive economic activity and a new way of doing business. What most commentators of the time missed, however, was that the Internet was not a creation of the U.S. government but rather an inevitable consequence of a business and consumer need created by a new phenomenon: mass computer storage.

ORIGINS OF ELECTRONIC DATA STORAGE

In the 1940s and 1950s, the U.S. Navy was undertaking a computer project titled "Whirlwind." Whirlwind was designed to support the development of flight simulations in support of pilot training.

While this would be an easy task today, it was revolutionary in many respects then. Most problems that were tackled using computers at that time were based on individual equations that needed to be applied many times (such as the repetitive calculation of artillery range tables). Flight simulations required complex algorithms with large amounts of data to be shared between the steps.

Apart from the many new and complex tasks involved, the output was time dependent. Until that time, all computing had been undertaken in batches with the only driver for speed being the time it took to get the final result.

The project was run by Jay W. Forrester who realized that existing technology was not able to deliver information to the flight-simulator environment quickly enough to be useful. He also realized that it wasn't processing power that was holding up the system; rather, it was the ability to access information from the archaic technologies in use at the time to store variables.

Forrester leveraged the work of An Wang, a physicist who was developing a technique to use magnetic fields to store individual bits of data. The high speed of this nonmechanical approach was exactly what Whirlwind needed. As a result of this collaboration, Wang's core memory (referred to as *core* because it uses the core magnetic fields) became the standard form of memory until the 1970s when silicon memory manufacture took over.

Previous forms of computer memory had been so inefficient that the concept of data was limited to variables explicitly set by the programmer at the time of computation. There was no need for any relationship to be described between any of these discrete variables.

With the introduction of core memory, however, digital computers could move into the mainstream of industry. They became business as well as mathematical tools capable of handling clerical, data-centric functions such as banking account balances, retail stock control, and financial ledgers.

Once the computer moved out of the purely mathematical world, the handling of complex data became possible, driving even greater storage needs, which in turn spawned developments in both memory and computer disk technologies. This insatiable need for data drove technological development at such a dramatic pace that cofounder of Intel Gordon Moore wrote in 1965:

> The complexity for minimum component costs has increased at a rate of roughly a factor of two per year ... Certainly over the short term this rate can be expected to continue, if not to increase. Over the longer term, the rate of increase is a bit more uncertain, although there is no reason to believe it will not remain nearly constant for at least 10 years. That means by 1975, the number of components per integrated circuit for minimum cost will be 65,000. I believe that such a large circuit can be built on a single wafer.[1]

This statement was later generalized into Moore's Law and extended by others to support the ongoing doubling every twelve to eighteen months of all types of computer storage and processing capacity.

STOCKS AND FLOWS

Economists deal with complex systems with elements that accumulate or reduce as a function of activity or time. The elements that accumulate are often referred to

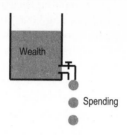

Figure 1.1   Stock of Wealth Reduced by Flow of Spending

as *stocks* because they represent an amount that builds up (a stock) and can be drawn from in the future. A good example of a stock is wealth. To accumulate or reduce a stock, something needs to be added or removed. This process is called a *flow*. Spending money is a good example of a flow because it reduces the stock of wealth (see Figure 1.1).

In the 1950s, the same Professor Jay W. Forrester who was central to the development of magnetic computer storage applied the principles of stocks and flows to create the discipline of *system dynamics*, which describes complex systems (of which the economy is a perfect example) by describing every element in terms of stocks or flows. The author has previously applied Forrester's principles of system dynamics to data warehouse systems in particular (see Hillard, Blecher, and O'Donnell, "The Implications of Chaos Theory on the Management of a Data Warehouse."[2] Chapter 9 introduces system dynamics and its application in more detail.

The Internet can be similarly described in terms of stocks and flows. Each server on the network accumulates information, while the routers direct the flow of information around the system.

Which is more valuable: the stock or the flow? Without the flow of the Internet, there is no ability to access information on individual servers. Without the stocks of information on the servers, there is no reason for the flow of the Internet to exist. Therefore, it can be said that stocks and flows are of equal value. To function, the Internet needs storage capacity and connectivity. Although the network technology for the information superhighway was available before the 1990s, the Internet did not come into existence until there were enough valuable stores of data that people wanted to access.

BUSINESS DATA

With the availability of practical technology for the storage of data, business enthusiastically adopted computing through the 1970s and 1980s; however, the cost of storage remained a substantial impediment to unfettered application and accumulation of business history. Computing historians can show this by many measures, but none is more dramatic than the rise of the Y2K problem when companies that had systems that were built during these years were so concerned with conserving storage that they reserved only two characters for the year of any date (e.g., *1985* became *85*).

By the end of the 1980s, Moore's Law began to catch up with the latent content generated by business. By the early 1990s, the price of semipermanent storage had reached the psychologically important threshold of US$1 per megabyte.

For the first time, business systems did not need to be so Spartan in deciding what data to keep. In fact, more and more programmers postponed the development of archive routines, knowing that Moore's Law would outpace the growth in their databases. Of even more benefit, business analysts could now require the collection of data that was ancillary to the core transaction, building up a context for every business relationship. The business system had become a data repository of value.

The Internet had existed in some form for decades, with the foundations laid in ARPANET in the 1970s and widely used local area networks (LANs) in the 1980s. The network technology was robust, but public and business interest in applying it further was limited by the lack of content. To leverage the stock and flow metaphor, there was no demand for the flow of information in the absence of any significant stocks of data.

Low-cost storage enabled the stocks of data to build in business and the wider community. Gradually hubs of content built up with proprietary access, such as bulletin boards, AOL (America On-Line), and many other similar services. The networking technology was mature and so it was inevitable that it would standardize.

A useful comparison is the introduction of telephones at the end of the nineteenth century. Initially, the technology was applied to pairs or to small numbers of businesses that needed to connect several of their locations. Even though the technology initially had some minor differences between suppliers, there was a very quick jump to exchanges and then interfaces between different exchanges. Today, we consider it historically inevitable that the telephone would quickly standardize to one network across the globe.

CHANGING BUSINESS MODELS

Historically, business has been heavily decentralized. A very good and illustrative example is the banking industry in which a bank branch manager in the 1970s and 1980s had considerable executive authority and prestige. The advent of centralized information has allowed the head office to take over the day-to-day running, approval, and review of transactions, ultimately leading to today's branch manager generally having a greatly reduced role and responsibility.

Access to complex information covering all aspects of business has coincided with a tectonic shift to centralized power and control in almost every industry sector, from retail through manufacturing, logistics, telecommunications, and financial services. Of course, one of the problems of this approach is the ability for small head-office errors to be magnified many times. An error in a ledger at a branch is limited to a small part of the business. A centralized error can be a material proportion of the business.

Robin Morgan, a feminist writer, once said that "Information is power." Armed for the first time with masses of information, head-office business executives have wielded previously unimaginable power, taking over not only broad strategy but the minutia of transaction review and approval. Morgan's hypothesis was that those armed with information are tempted to conceal it from others and use it to exercise control. Many staff in large organizations today regularly complain about their access to information and the lack of discretion they are permitted in the fulfillment of their jobs. The excuse most commonly given for the concealment of information is market regulation (such as the prohibition of insider trading) or commercial sensitivities (such as those used by government to avoid disclosing dealings with the private sector).

It is worth considering whether the reason some information is hidden from wider view may be due to a lack of confidence in its quality. This is particularly relevant if published results are derived from the detail and there could be a genuine fear that independent analysis (even within their own ranks) of the data could yield different and challenging results.

The question that any organization needs to ask itself is whether it is using information to create the most dynamic, responsive, and adaptable enterprise possible, or is it using information to satisfy the need for power by a privileged few?

INFORMATION SHARING VERSUS INFRASTRUCTURE SHARING

Companies, like any social network, gain scale because there is an advantage to their constituent parts. Companies, like countries, break apart when the constituent parts are able to realize more value without the parent entity.

During the majority of the twentieth century, conglomerates formed with the express purpose of providing back-end and management scale. By being part of the one entity, constituent businesses were able to share capital, administration services, logistic hubs, office space, and other traditional infrastructure. Business trends through the last decades have created third-party services that can provide such facilities more effectively and usually more cheaply than in-house equivalents.

The growth of superannuation and other pension funds has created cash box investments looking to provide working capital for high-growth business.

Large-scale services firms have standardized the provision of administrative services such as payroll, accounts, and even more hands-on services such as call centers.

The privatization of traditional postal services is combined with much more entrepreneurial transport businesses to provide outsourced warehousing, distribution, and global integration at unit costs that are less than anything available to even the largest conglomerate.

Commercial office space is much more commoditized with a mobile workforce that expects the facilities in the location or locations that they choose to work rather than an employer who requires them to relocate daily to a supercampus.

In short, the infrastructural reasons for conglomerate businesses to exist have been dramatically reduced over time and the capital markets punish companies that have failed to realize this.

There is, however, a new and even more powerful reason for conglomerate companies to exist. While they are more complex to manage than their simplified competitors, they also have access to equally complex data about their stakeholders and operations. To justify its existence, a conglomerate cannot rely on back-end infrastructure sharing; rather, it must be able to demonstrate that it is generating growth and cash flow through active sharing of information between every division of its constituent businesses. It can only demonstrate this effectively to its stakeholders by measuring the equivalent of gross domestic product (GDP) in the terms of its own internal information economy.

There is no better example of this than the attempts by media companies, such as Rupert Murdoch's News Corporation, to establish their role in the information economy. Small media companies see the Internet as an opportunity to get their product to market without needing expensive infrastructure. Large companies like News Corporation need to find a way to use their extensive content to aggregate more effectively and offer consumers a product for which they are prepared to pay a premium.

GOVERNING THE NEW BUSINESS

Like *information economy*, the term *information governance* has been misused and misunderstood. Most organizations, pressed by regulatory compliance or other oversight, have introduced some form of information governance, but in general it is seen as a committee-based audit process resulting in some score and identification of issues to be resolved.

Human review and intervention is seldom sustainable without permanent intervention by an outside authority. Even when this happens, in the absence of a crisis, the review becomes superficial and compliance driven.

To use information to achieve business outcomes, organizations need to motivate their staff to use information for the greater good of the organization rather than for individual gain or power. Using Forrester's stocks and flows metaphor of the enterprise, it would appear that if the only use of information is to cement power, then information will naturally flow into a few locations without natural dissemination to the wider enterprise.

Centralized and mandated initiatives seldom work, with most economists agreeing that groups will seek to serve the greater good only when there is a currency that they are exchanging and that results in some type of personal gain (even if it is only in terms of credit or well-being). For this reason, the business that seeks to model itself to achieve its business goals must assign value for information and, even more important, a currency to recognize its exchange. Information is neither free nor unlimited.

It is the role of information governance to track the creation of information, understand the value it provides to the organization, reward its sharing, and understand its depreciation through use or time. It should come as no surprise that many of the activities of information governance are founded in economics and the management of the information economy.

Information governance and information management are sometimes confused. Information governance is concerned with supervising and motivating information activities without necessarily accessing the content. Information management describes the activities themselves and involves directly interacting with the information materials.

Chapter 3 tackles this challenge in detail, including using the concept of an "information currency" as a way to challenge existing business models and more effectively leverage the information asset.

While it is simple to understand, monetary value is often not enough to reward information exchange. Information budgets (a little like the carbon credits proposed in response to global warming) allow groups to become experts in the generation of relevant content. Breaking the budget into strategic categories allows the company to build a balanced approach to its business goals and encourages exchange between departments to meet targets in each of the relevant categories.

Unfortunately, the internal information economy is too complex for a small number of universal rules to be applied universally across the enterprise. Markets are required at the individual product line level. For instance, the sharing of data about a customer across product groups (such as is found in telecommunications or financial services companies) requires a benefit to flow between them. Since the objective is to reward further business, such a motivation could be achieved by aligning permitted customer discounts to the sharing of detailed customer data. (Information governance and information currency are described further in Chapter 3.)

SUCCESS IN THE INFORMATION ECONOMY

If the reader is willing to accept the premise that content is more important than transmission (i.e., stocks are more important than flows), and considers carefully if information is being used to better the enterprise rather than control it, then it is possible to begin to look at organizational success in terms of the information economy.

The first step is to understand what *success* actually means. It isn't obvious because every organization has its own objectives. For a government enterprise, success is usually defined in terms of service or public good. For a company or other type of firm, success has to be aligned to strategic goals, such as positioning for future growth, extracting maximum cash flow from an asset, or responding to disruptive competitive events in the market. In each of these cases, information is critical but how it is used will differ. When the enterprise's business goals are understood, decisions can then be made about how information should be used, as shown in the following examples.

> The company that is trying to maximize cash flow, for instance, is likely to put a high priority on discipline and will not foster innovation at the frontline (after all, the main obstacle to maximizing cash is its diversion to new initiatives). This type of organization will usually use information most effectively to drive centralized control by a small number of business executives.
>
> The government enterprise that is seeking to maximize its stakeholder (public) service will often seek to use information to empower individual line service staff to make the right decision for their direct client while at the same time monitoring compliance with government policy and good budgetary discipline.
>
> The firm that is seeking to differentiate through innovation will try to maximize its business talent pool by creating a culture of collaboration across the business that is not dependent on hierarchy. In a meritocracy, business leaders must be prepared to promote initiatives that they find neither intuitive nor comfortable but that are thoroughly examined through modeling and peer review.

Each of the preceding examples is a generalization and represents only a subset of the possible permutations of business need and the application of information. If the reader understands how information should be applied to achieve his or her strategic goals within an organization, then the next question to ask is how can these principles be introduced and governed? The answer is a properly structured internal economy based on an information currency and appropriate governance.

NOTES

1. Gordon E. Moore (1965), "Cramming More Components onto Integrated Circuits," *Electronics Magazine*, 38(8).
2. R. Hillard, P. Blecher, and P. O'Donnell (1999). "The Implications of Chaos Theory on the Management of a Data Warehouse," Proceedings of the International Society of Decision Support Systems (ISDSS).

Chapter 2

The Language of Information

The study of any subject has to start with an introduction to the vernacular of the discipline. In chemistry, this means understanding the periodic table, in mathematics the language of algebra, in accounting it means understanding the meaning of price-to-earnings ratios, amortization, depreciation, and so on.

In the discipline of information management there are still many different ways of describing information, including the meaning of terms like *metadata* and *document*. Because much of the field has developed rapidly in response to new technologies, there has been no opportunity for a consensus on definitions, terms, and language to develop.

One of the more succinct definitions of information has been suggested by Robert M. Losee[1] and will be discussed in more detail in Chapter 6:

> Information is produced by all processes and it is the values of characteristics in the processes' output that are information.

Without a common definition, practitioners who work with information in different disciplines as diverse as computer science, communications, and library management don't have a linguistic foundation to support important discussions around the content that overlaps all of their areas of expertise. Over time, many aspects of the language associated with information management need to be standardized by professional consensus.

The current lack of a common language is a significant issue faced by the information management profession. Because practitioners have few standards they can use when discussing information concepts, there is little cross-pollination of ideas among the different domains of information management. Compare this to the field of accounting, in which the same principles are applied across industries and accounting specializations.

In information management, there have been some ambitious and in a couple of cases, very successful, attempts to provide languages in specific domains. However, these efforts are largely immature and the field is waiting for practitioners to reach consensus and this takes time.

There are a wide range of stakeholders in such a language. The librarian profession is responsible for information storage and retrieval for both corporate clients and the general public. Communications engineers develop solutions that transmit messages between machines and people. Data modelers design database structures that hold operational and analytical data for many corporate applications. Chief data officers and data stewards manage the corporate information asset on behalf of the business. Chief information officers and technology managers look after the computer systems that store and retrieve the data. Knowledge managers act as corporate information coaches, helping organizations to realize the breadth of their capabilities and reduce their dependencies on individuals.

Before the widely disparate groups of professionals can agree on a common language, they must establish a foundation for how to differentiate data, information, and knowledge. At present, there is not even agreement about whether the word *data* is singular or plural with popular and academic use differing in some countries.

The word *data* is derived from Latin and is the plural of *datum*. The word *datum* has a long heritage in the English language and continues to be used by many disciplines, such as surveying and engineering, to mean a reference point. This appears to be the historical reason that the word *datum* is seldom used in the context of information management. To avoid confusion, it is advisable not to use the word *datum* in the context of information management.

The debate about whether *data* should be treated as plural or singular is ongoing. Language scholars appear to have a preference for the plural form, for example:

These data were retrieved from the computer.

Such an approach is often used in general language in the United States, but it appears to be less common in countries that derive their English more directly from Britain. Overall, the most common use appears to assume that *data* is a singular mass noun, similar to *water*, thus the following two sentences are in the same structure:

The water was retrieved from the bucket.

The data was retrieved from the computer.

Given that *information* is a singular mass noun and is consistent with the growing consensus on *data*, it is likely that this form will prevail.

The use of the word *knowledge* in the context of information usually refers to codifying interpretations of data. *Knowledge* is generally subjective, interpretive, and depends on the experiences of the organization and the individual.

The discipline of Knowledge Management, which is definitely a branch of Information Management, has two distinct types of knowledge: tacit and explicit. *Tacit knowledge* is commonly understood, often regarded as obvious but is difficult to describe in a proscriptive manner. *Explicit knowledge*, on the other hand, is clear and often has parameters that can be recorded. For example, a group of sales staff

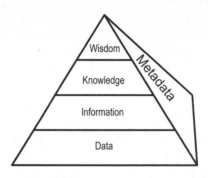

Figure 2.1   Wisdom or Knowledge Pyramid

may exercise their judgment on when to offer a discount to potential customers—the judgment they make is not documented and is based on their tacit knowledge of when it will have the most impact on the potential sale. In another organization, the decision on discounting might be clearly documented and applied based on specific volume thresholds, in this case the knowledge on when to apply the discount is described as being explicit.

During the 1980s, computer-based trading became popular. Some investment funds promoted themselves as using such an approach exclusively. One of the reasons it was attractive to investors was that the decision-making process of fund managers has often been based on tacit knowledge, which is difficult to quantify. By moving to a rules-based algorithm, the investment knowledge became explicit. While still used to a large extent today, the use of automated algorithms is almost always paired with the tacit knowledge of an expert, as the global stock market crash of 1987 taught investors that there is significant value in tacit knowledge that is too complex to codify as explicit knowledge.

Conventional knowledge management definitions imply that information is derived from data and that knowledge is derived from information. This is sometimes described in terms of a pyramid, as shown in Figure 2.1. As shown in this diagram, some practitioners have gone further and are defining wisdom in terms of its derivation from knowledge. It isn't known who first drew the pyramid in this way, but it has been popular for many years.

Such a pyramid could be used, for instance, to illustrate the decision-making process used by a department store to buy next season's fashions. In this example, the raw data could correspond to the retail sales transactions associated with existing merchandise. The information might be this data into sales performance by color and style. Explicit knowledge, based on this information, can be the apportionment of sizes based on the sales trend information. Finally, wisdom can take many forms including insight into whether it is possible to draw conclusions on next year's fashion demand based on this year's sales.

It is interesting that T.S. Eliot appears to have anticipated this discussion more than half a century beforehand:

Where is the wisdom we have lost in knowledge?

Where is the knowledge we have lost in information?[2]

While the inclusion of wisdom is very appealing, it is difficult to describe in a meaningful way and little, if any, direct benefit has been gained from having it in this type of model. For that reason, the loose concept of wisdom is not widely regarded as being a legitimate component of information management.

The relationship between knowledge and information is useful. It provides an explicit description of the role of both tacit and explicit knowledge in realizing the economic benefit of the information asset. The relationship between information and data is much more troubling given the lack of a clear differentiation between the two concepts.

There is a tendency by most people to generically talk about information when referring to anything that *informs*, whether it be a raw set of numbers or a spreadsheet document, with an advanced level of interpretation. It would be extremely arrogant for a profession that hasn't even got its scope or definition defined to try and mandate a change to the popular usage of the term *information*.

Broadly, it appears that popular usage is that *data* means a set of numbers or a very unprocessed list of textual items. *Information* is an umbrella that includes data together with all documents, Web pages, and anything else that is absorbed by the senses through a computer interface. Although it is implied, there is no requirement in any widely accepted definition that information be derived from data.

Although both *data* and *information* are generally mass nouns, there are still many different ways of describing specific collections of data and information. In statistics, such a collection is called a *set*. In database theory, a logical grouping is called an *entity* and a physical grouping is called a *table*. In its raw form, when extracted from a table, the grouping becomes known as a *data set*. In content and knowledge management, the most common grouping is a *document*. In communications, engineers think about data being combined into *messages*.

STRUCTURED QUERY LANGUAGE

There is a way of phrasing questions about data contained in structured databases. It is called structured query language (SQL) and is officially pronounced *es queue el*. The language was developed during the 1970s and is directly derived from Edgar F. Codd's 1970 original paper and model,[3] which will be discussed more fully in Chapter 4.

SQL has a structure that is defined by identifying collections of data. The identification verb is *SELECT* followed by nouns for each of the information attributes that are required, followed by a *FROM* preposition, which defines the source entity/ table. For example:

SELECT name, address, phone FROM customer

If only a subset of entries is required from customer the adverb *WHERE* filter can be added:

SELECT name, address, phone FROM customer WHERE gender = "MALE"

The simplicity of SQL hides its elegant power. For instance, these three primary terms, when applied properly, allow for the creation of data sets that draw from more than one table at a time. They are, however, well short of a full language to describe data. For instance, not every question can be described in terms of one SQL statement, which has led to a proliferation of proprietary languages that embed SQL concepts.

The biggest drawback of SQL, though, is that it is cumbersome for nonprogrammers to use, making it a technical rather than business language. Even practitioners who are very familiar with SQL find that it is not sufficiently intuitive to explain the meaning of a particular question without careful examination.

With the disbanding of standards oversight of SQL, the vendor community has taken over the definition and self-certification of compatibility. Even a copy of the full SQL standard is no longer available as a free resource.

STATISTICS

Statistics is simply a form of applied mathematics that has a specific language that allows different practitioners to compare results. By its very nature, most statistical problems deal with measuring degrees of uncertainty. With its different types of tests and methods to measure levels of confidence, the language of statistics allows professional statisticians to compare results and understand exactly why a particular interpretation has been made of a given data set.

In the field of statistics, data sets have parameters. They are either a sample or represent the entire population. Each sample and population data set can be described in terms of their *members, mean, median, standard deviation*, and other related terms. Any statistician who looks at these terms is immediately comfortable with their meanings and with the descriptions and assumptions being made about the data set.

Broadly, the language of statistics is broken into two parts. The first describes the sample and/or population with, arguably, the key parameters being the population mean, median, and standard deviation. The second describes tests or hypotheses that have been applied to the data set. The key parameters of tests include the probability, standard error, and *p*-value, which equates to the test confidence.

XQUERY LANGUAGE

With more and more data being represented in eXtensible Mark-up Language (XML), there is a push to bring together SQL, XML, and statistical principles into a single language. In theory, even large databases can be projected from relational databases into XML format leaving them open to direct query.

The XQuery standard, unlike SQL, is being developed by an open committee of the W3C (the standards governing committee of the World Wide Web). The standard overlaps with another XML language, eXtensible Stylesheet Language Transformations (XSLT), which supports complex XML transformations. XQuery, however, is focused on using the principles of relational algebra and applying them to repositories of XML documents.

Over time, XQuery has the potential to be widely adopted, making it a standard for static data sets used in statistics, accessing structured data in databases, and manipulating documents of text and spreadsheets that are increasingly being stored in the XML format. At the time of writing, this is a future objective that is a long way from reality.

SPREADSHEETS

Despite the maturing of information technology and the advent of enterprise resource planning (ERP), an increasing volume of critical business data is being held in spreadsheets. Many organizations are finding that there are hundreds if not thousands of individual spreadsheets involved in the production of business reports. While the back-end systems might contain more data than ever before, the complexity of the metrics demanded by executive management and boards continues to outpace improvements by the technology team.

With such a dependence on the spreadsheet, it is disturbing that the language of this toolset is largely limited to coordinate referencing in the form of columns, rows, and pages (with the introduction of tabbed spreadsheets).

Currently, the spreadsheet market is dominated by Microsoft's Excel, which provides a built-in and proprietary control language, including functions to cross-reference and calculate results. Beyond such proprietary tools, there is very little in the way of standards to describe or navigate the content of a spreadsheet.

Most users of spreadsheets appear unaware that there is a gap in their language. A comparison with the more mature domain of statistics illustrates the issue. In statistics, there are parameters that can be applied to data. There are no similar standards or conventions for spreadsheets. For instance, it is not immediately obvious where an individual cell has been sourced from, with the options including being directly entered on the worksheet, derived from another cell, cut and pasted from another location, or directly linked to a different data source such as another spreadsheet or a database. In some organizations, arbitrary rules are being applied to provide this type of metadata visually.

There are also no error or confidence conventions provided by spreadsheet vendors (e.g., Microsoft Excel) as there are with statistical data standards and software packages. This is surprising given that the best estimate of spreadsheet error rates indicates that approximately 5 percent of all cells are in some way incorrect either in the data they hold or the formula used to calculate the result.[4]

DOCUMENTS AND WEB PAGES

A large amount of information, and particularly knowledge, is described in narrative form within documents. Librarians interested in information management readily fall back on the Dewey Decimal System to catalog and locate individual works of nonfiction. Such an approach is rarely used in a corporate environment, particularly with documents that are internally authored and subject to ongoing change.

In Chapter 7, approaches to classifying documents using metadata standards are introduced but they will not enter popular usage in the near future. The advantage that such metadata does have, however, is that the designers of these standards have ensured that they remain openly available at no cost and are easily understood by most users.

Most authors and users of documents, however, make the assumption that text is a static item with the concept of sections, headings, paragraphs, and sentences cascading in a hierarchy, very much like the early data management systems. With the Web, however, narrative, text, and in fact almost any content is hardly ever completely static.

Electronic wikis (such as the one that powers the well-known Wikipedia) and other similar online technologies have introduced dynamic documents that are updated in real time to match the environments they are commenting on. Further, the concept of *transclusion* has matured since its original introduction by Ted Nelson in 1981.[5] While most users of hypertext are comfortable with the concept of cross-referencing and hyperlinks, transclusion introduces the concept that entire bodies of narrative, diagrams, and structured data can be duplicated within a separate document.

Transclusion has the potential to change the way that documents are used, as paragraphs take on the properties of programmatic objects and are able to be reused without clumsy referencing, making a piece of narrative flow. Such a change also has the effect of forcing authors to be much more structured in the way they approach their documents.

Many practitioners are also looking in the future to the concept of the *semantic web* to structure content, particularly material on the Web, in such a way that it is more easily found, aggregated for new purposes, and integrated very much like structured data. The challenge the semantic Web faces is the need for the site authors to invest additional effort without necessarily knowing if it is going to be of value to their readers.

KNOWLEDGE, COMMUNICATIONS, AND INFORMATION THEORY

While the discipline of Knowledge Management is under the umbrella of Information Management, the language of knowledge lacks common standards or wide agreement among practitioners. While many in the field see knowledge as being the highest level in the pyramid (if wisdom is discounted as undefined), it is arguable that it has the closest relationship of any aspect of information management to communications engineering and its underlying Information Theory.

Information Theory began as a discipline to formalize the communications technologies, starting with the telegraph and moving through telephony, radio, and ultimately to digital communications. As is described in Chapter 6, Claude Shannon's work in this field has formed the basis of the entire Information Management discipline and has had an impact well beyond the narrow domain for communications. Shannon simplifies communications to a single model shown in Figure 2.2.

With this model, Shannon effectively duplicated quantum theory by making the content and observation part of the science of communications. To maximize the use of a channel, it becomes important to understand the content and how it is interpreted by both the sender and receiver. In other words, the communications engineer cannot ignore the meaning of the message or the knowledge that is gained by the receiver.

Bob Losee provides a model to describe the role of knowledge more formally as part of the process of encoding a message.[6] He proposes that knowledge is encoded in narrative phrases that are ultimately broken down into the building blocks of language in phonemes. Such a model generalizes knowledge and communications in a way that can ultimately be independent of the language spoken.

If x represents a concept then its complete communication is completed by converting it to its underlying phrases and phonemes that can be transmitted in an abstract form and re-created into phonemes and phrases that make sense to the receiver in the form:

$$phrase\left(phoneme\left(phoneme^{-1}\left(phrase^{-1}\left(x\right)\right)\right)\right)$$

As with documents, while these concepts are powerful they are a long way from universal acceptance or standardized terminology.

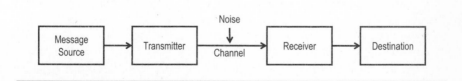

Figure 2.2   Shannon's Channel Model

NOTES

1. R. M. Losee (1997), "A Discipline Independent Definition of Information," *Journal of the American Society of Information Science*, 48(3): 254–69.

2. T. S. Eliot (1934), *The Rock* (NY: Faber & Faber).

3. E. F. Codd, (1970), "A Relational Model of Data for Large Shared Data Banks," *CACM* 13(6).

4. R. R. Panko (January 2005), "What We Know about Spreadsheet Errors." Available at http://panko.cba.hawaii.edu/ssr/whatknow.htm.

5. T. Nelson (1981), *Literary Machines* (Sausalito, California: Mindful Press).

6. R. M. Losee (1997), "A Discipline Independent Definition of Information," *Journal of the American Society of Information Science*, 48(3): 254–69.

Chapter 3

Information Governance

Prior to the 1990s, large business relied heavily on its group financial ledger to integrate information across the company. Evidence of this can be seen in historical reporting (such as annual reports) from the era in which financial results are the main statement of the health of the company.

With the advent of much larger volumes of information, twenty-first-century reports still use the language of the financial ledger, but these reports now include much more sophisticated metrics. For instance, retailers can now provide information to shareholders about the comparable store sales by individual merchandise categories and mergers are able to be measured in detail as facilities are aggregated or realigned.

Just as dramatically, the advent of real-time information from operational processes across the enterprise has meant that it is possible for centralized executive management to apply direct control over a much wider scope of operation. This is one of the factors that have resulted in the consolidation of many businesses into much larger global operations.

During most of the twentieth century when management was undertaken as a hands-on exercise, human senses were the main vehicle for data collection. Executives could see if the factory floor was busy or note how many shoppers were walking the aisles. As business has gone global, teams are often virtual, with communication impeded by time zones, language, and national and organizational culture.

This means that information is the glue that holds the organization together. Governing information is, in a very real sense, about governing the business as a whole.

INFORMATION CURRENCY

To use information to achieve business outcomes, organizations need to motivate their staff to use information for the good of the organization rather than for their own individual gain or power. For this reason, the organization that seeks to achieve its business goals through the better use of information must not only estimate value but also allow for its internal (and ultimately external) trade using an agreed currency to recognize its exchange. Information is neither free nor unlimited.

The simplest form of currency is money. A monetary value placed on each data set allows for its exchange with a flow of assigned capital through the organization.

The business unit or department that buys the content needs to achieve an economic return that is greater than the Treasury-assigned rate. The selling department can use the same capital to invest in plant and equipment or make further purchases of information.

While simple to understand, monetary value is often not enough to reward information exchange. Information budgets (a little like the carbon credits proposed in response to global warming) allow groups to become experts in the generation of relevant content. Breaking the budget into strategic categories allows the company to build a balanced approach to its business goals and encourages exchange between departments to meet targets in each of the relevant categories.

Unfortunately, the internal information economy is not so simple that a small number of rules can be applied universally across the enterprise. Markets are required at the individual product line level. For instance, the sharing of data about a customer across product groups (such as is found in telecommunications or financial services companies) requires a benefit to flow between the groups.

For example, a customer walks into a bank branch to inquire about a home loan. Marketing professionals involved in the financial services industry know that the complexity of this type of product often influences the decision with the customer deciding to take up an offer to provide a loan because there is so much work involved in visiting multiple branches and understanding different product alternatives. This is one of the reasons why so many banks are opening more branches, discouraging an Internet-only approach to sales, and trying to remove mortgage brokers from the equation. Because of the complexity of the product the bank knows that a customer who has taken the time to visit a bank branch to understand a home loan product is very likely to accept an offer made to them without extensive comparative research. The lifetime value of the loan that the customer is seeking can be calculated, which is proportional to the value of the information gained from the customer.

In most organizations, whoever deals with the customer first tries to take credit for their business, particularly if commission is payable. If, however, the information value is credited to the line staff members' budget when they make information available to the wider organization then they will be encouraged to do so rather than try to hold all of the business for themselves.

Engineering the business through the value of the information is an enormously powerful approach to grow the customer relationship because the detailed information provided by the customer visiting the branch is likely to contain insights of great value to other bank-promoting products such as savings accounts, credit cards, and home insurance. However, this information should not be treated as free. There are only so many ways that the same information can be used before its value is diminished. The commonsense way of understanding this is to think in terms of the customer's reaction to the data being used. If the customer is contacted by one or two arms of the bank with very targeted offers that directly reflect the needs that he or she has expressed, there is a strong probability that he or she will be interested in the offer. If the customer is contacted by too many different parts of the bank or too often, he or she will simply decline all offers without looking at them closely.

If the information can only be used a certain number of times, it can be assumed to have a finite value. That finite value should be spent wisely on behalf of the shareholders who own the information asset.

ECONOMIC VALUE OF DATA

Economists know that currency is a proxy for value and simply facilitates its trade.

Before developing an approach to information governance, it is important to get some kind of understanding of the value of the information asset. While there is increasing awareness that information is an asset, attempts to value the information have not been standardized or widely accepted by accounting bodies.

With information management and leverage comes the ability for knowledge workers (such as actuaries, investment bankers, product researchers, and analysts) to make fact-based decisions. The information that they use to make decisions and the processes that allow them to leverage that information have an intrinsic value to the organization that is seldom fully recognized.

Programs aiming to leverage information (typically under banners such as Data Warehousing or Management Information) often struggle to determine the potential return on investment. Calculations are typically based on either specific process improvements or anticipated organization growth.

A top-down approach is the only realistic means to identify the return that could potentially be achieved given the size of this intangible asset and this provides a target that the stakeholder teams should aim to achieve.

In general, information is seen in terms of its application. A product has an asset value associated with its goodwill, utility, or product rate of return. In addition, the market often values information in its own right.

The starting point is the total market value of the entity itself. For stand-alone public companies, this is an absolute in terms of the total shares and their current price for commercial entities. For divisions of larger entities, it can usually be estimated on a realistic basis such as the proportion of the balance sheet. For non-profit or government entities it is harder, but not impossible, to determine a realistic value. The total market value is typically the price that the market places on a company assuming no merger and acquisition activity occurs (unless there is specific market speculation).

The next step is the most difficult. Determine how an independent third party (such as a potential buyer) would value the organization if it was offered without historical information about its products, customers, staff, and risk. This is a difficult exercise because it must be assumed that sufficient information and knowledge is retained to meet minimum regulatory and operational requirements, but for the purposes of our experiment we can assume that the split is possible.

Table 3.1 Estimated Proportion of Value Related to Information

Sector	Proportion of Value Tied Up in Information
Simple manufacturing	30–40%
Telecommunications, utilities, and other infrastructure-related services	50–60%
Complex intangible service companies such as financial services	70–80%
Resources sector providers	40–60%

It may be helpful to look at the major products of business processes and consider the role of information repositories in order to determine value. Typically, highly process-oriented businesses dealing in physical infrastructure (such as manufacturers) have the lowest scores but they still find that at least one-third of their underlying value comes from the corporate repositories of information that they hold on supply chain, manufacturing formulas, and customer buying history. Entities that provide complex services or other intangible products, such as financial providers, find that the majority of their capability comes from information in one form or another. A simple rule of thumb based on experience is listed in Table 3.1.

The values estimated for Table 3.1 are intended only to be indicative and are not the result of any detailed research. The intention is to show the order of magnitude of the value of information as a proportion of organizational value based on experience.

For instance, using the estimates in Table 3.1, this would mean that a bank with a market value of $10 billion has of the order of $7 billion to $8 billion in information and knowledge assets, including product intellectual property. For government and nonprofit entities, a meaningful value can still be estimated by comparing the services provided to those that could be outsourced or purchased from the private sector and then estimating the cost of buying those entities.

With an overall value estimated, the value should then be divided between the divisions (based on asset values, contribution, or other appropriate metrics) and further divided across the business functions as a proportion contribution (note that this division should include both profit and cost centers).

With the information value now assigned by process, the final step is to estimate how this divides between the data sets that support each process. Note that individual data sets can support more than one process and the value is aggregative.

One final note: To understand the size of opportunity is to consider the annual depreciation of the information asset. Information is just like any other asset; without further investment it depreciates every year at a definable rate.

Information diminishes in value as its quality and usability deteriorates over a period of time. The information that an organization holds changes continuously. For instance, one study found that customer information such as address or e-mail changes at a rate of more than 10 percent per month.[1] This could be caused by people moving locations, links being broken, modified product information, and changes in employee roles. Information depreciates for a variety of reasons and includes aspects such as being superseded by newer and more up-to-date information, users being unaware that the information exists, and also the inability to access the information due to access rights.

The implication is that data deteriorates or expires over time unless it is kept current. Since data is the basis for information, the assumption can therefore be extrapolated to apply to the entire information asset. A conservative estimate, if there is no action to curb the deterioration, is that this deterioration or depreciation occurs at a rate of at least 20 percent per annum. Therefore, in the example of a company with information assets worth $10 billion, without intervention at least $1 billion per annum is wiped from the value of this asset.

Of course for almost all organizations, we know the information asset is increasing and not decreasing in value. The assumption can safely be made that substantial investment is being made solely in the management of information. The investment is not referring to the information technology cost but rather the total investment in and managing the information completely independent of the cost of running the systems.

GOALS OF INFORMATION GOVERNANCE

Recognizing the need to derive value from the information asset, a set of principles, a strategy, and an approach to governance is required. The first step is the development of an information governance charter. Such a charter needs to be embraced by the board or its equivalent and have a set of information principles that are aligned to the strategic goals and recognizes the structural tensions that exist in every organization.

The following six principles are a good starting point for such a charter:

Principle 1: Fact-based decision making. The first and most important information principle is that the information asset should be leveraged every day in every decision. Both strategic and operational decisions should be based on facts that can be sourced back to data that is held by the enterprise.

Principle 2: Integrated data with consistent definitions. Accepting that an organization's major asset is information, there is no value in each unit of the enterprise being part of the whole unless it is able to leverage that enterprise asset in an integrated and synergistic way (i.e., the whole is greater than the sum of parts).

Principle 3: Appropriate retention of detailed data. Information should be retained whenever physically possible within the constraints of government legislation, corporate ethics, and privacy commitments.

Principle 4: Quality of data will be measured. Data quality is relative to the purpose to which it is to be applied. Decision makers not only need access to data, but more important, they also need to understand the timing, reconciliation, completeness, and accuracy of that data. Data quality is neither abstract nor qualitative; rather, it should be measured in absolute terms.

Principle 5: Appropriate enterprise access. Staff are a valued and trusted resource to the company. By default, every member of staff can be trusted to handle information appropriately and sensitively. The default position is that a staff member can access information unless there is a specific commercial, legal, or ethical reason why the information should not be made available to this individual.

Principle 6: Every data item has one person or role as ultimate custodian. Every item of data requires unique and ultimate ownership by a single role and person. This does not imply that all customers, products, or other items of data maintain common ownership; rather, it means that a matrix of responsibilities should be managed that ensures that issues or conflicts always have an ultimate point of escalation.[2]

Regardless of organizational culture or dynamics, once the board is convinced of the necessity of focusing on information and its governance, one or more people need to be given the authority and accountability to implement the charter and realize the goals of information management.

In many organizations, such a role is increasingly being called names like the chief data officer (CDO). The CDO or equivalent position should have real accountability and may exist at either or both of the group and the divisional levels depending on the culture and strength of the bonds between the business units.

The principles become the key performance indicators (KPIs) of the role and the budgets should include an element expressed in terms of the selected information currencies. Apart from the authority that the role needs to carry though a senior executive reporting line, the office of the CDO should have a direct accountability to the board and specifically the audit subcommittee or its equivalent.

ORGANIZATIONAL MODELS

The approach to information governance, roles, and principles needs to be tailored to the organization structure in place. As a broad generalization, organizations fall into three structures.

The first structure (shown in Figure 3.1) is a functional structure with a chief executive officer (CEO) and a team of executives managing the different business

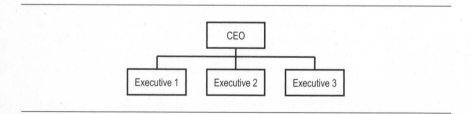

Figure 3.1   Functional Structure

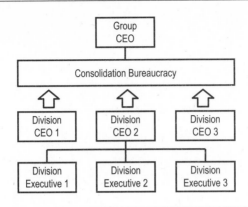

Figure 3.2 Divisional Structure

departments, such as finance, sales, research, manufacturing, and information technology. This organizational model is usually the first one adopted by both commercial and public sector businesses.

The second structure (shown in Figure 3.2) is a divisional structure that is usually adopted to solve the problems of growth and increasing complexity. Each division is governed with a leadership team that reports to a groupwide executive team. The consolidated group usually develops a bureaucracy of its own to manage the integration of the divisions. The scope of the division varies, with some being geographic, others being product related, and yet others based on the type of customer group being served.

As organizations grow larger, they find that the divisions become increasingly autonomous and fail to leverage the resources of their siblings. Such resources could include customers, product expertise, or infrastructure. This often leads to a matrix structure in which the shared resources are centralized with their own lines of management who provide services into each of the divisions. Inevitably, this leads to a tension (sometimes healthy and often not) between the power and control of the matrix lines (see Figure 3.3).

Organizational Theory continues to evolve with new organic and network structures being added all the time, but at their heart these three concepts mirror the evolution of information in the enterprise.

Initially, information is directly tied to business functions, with different lines of business directly accessing information from each other's portfolios when required. This is possible when the size of the enterprise is limited.

With growth comes a group bureaucracy. At this point, the lines of business become significantly separated and the sharing of information and other resources becomes much more difficult. This leads to the matrix structure that permits the reintroduction of better resource sharing including information.

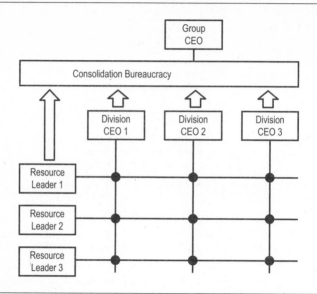

Figure 3.3   Matrix Structure

In the functional structure, the role of CDO can reside with one of the functions and needs to have a voice at the executive team level. Because the organization is usually fairly tightly integrated, the CEO's mandate alone is usually enough to empower the role and the functions of the role.

In the divisional structure, it is not enough to have a CDO as part of the group bureaucracy. There needs to be accountability for the charter of information governance within each division. Inevitably, the divisional structure will result in isolated stores of data; however, the extent to which data is isolated can be managed by effective standards and the use of the Small Worlds and related techniques (discussed in Chapter 5).

In the matrix structure, the opportunity exists to reintegrate the information functions into a horizontal shared resource under the command of the CDO.

OWNERSHIP OF INFORMATION

Information belongs to the shareholders or other stakeholders of the organization. The business is its custodian and needs to take this responsibility seriously. While a CDO is a key role within the enterprise, it should not be solely responsible for the content.

Business functions need to take ownership for data sets with an accountability derived from the principles of the information governance charter. Consequences for failure should be modeled on the scenario of errors appearing in the financial accounts (something for which the CFO would be directly accountable).

The concept of data ownership is not a technology function and should reside at senior levels (ideally the executive suite) so that the accountability can be reported directly to the board, including the audit subcommittee or its equivalent.

Recruitment to the ownership role needs to take account of the real work that needs to be done by providing both budget and rewards. The opportunities to the business, and hence the individual, need to be clearly described in terms of leveraging the information asset in new and creative ways.

STRATEGIC VALUE MODELS

To tailor the role of information governance in the different organizational models, it is important to align the charter with the strategic goals of the enterprise. While organizations' objectives often appear similar, their stage in their own life cycles can mean that each entity has different goals. Even shareholder-owned companies are not all identical, with some chasing quick capital growth while others are trying to maximize revenue and some are even simply trying to minimize their rate of decline.

To understand how information is best able to be leveraged, it is useful to consider organizational objectives in five dimensions: growth, innovation, complexity, agility, and investment. These five dimensions are designed to map strategic goals to an information governance charter (see Figure 3.4).

The *growth* dimension considers how the organization is planning to increase in scale. In business, this equates to activities like introducing new products, achieving greater market share, or acquiring another entity. Often, this is expressed simply as increasing the balance sheet or market capitalization. In the public sector, this

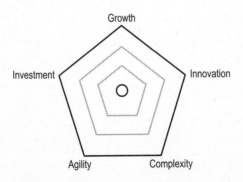

Figure 3.4 Organization Goals as They Impact Information Management

can mean implementing new government programs, merging with another department, or increasing general service to the public.

The *innovation* dimension considers how the organization embraces new and innovative thinking. Some enterprises value radical endeavors; others prefer to let their cohort do the heavy lifting and class themselves as fast followers; and a final group would rather extract maximum value from their existing products or services and avoid embracing change.

The *complexity* dimension interprets the value and differentiation that the organization seeks to extract from the sophisticated nature of their processes or product offerings. Some businesses value the intricate nature of their organization as a barrier to their competitors while others see it as the cause of overheads and seek to streamline processes at the expense of breadth of offering.

Different industries and government policy sectors change at different rates. Their *agility* factor, or their ability to respond rapidly to (or even driving) changes in their environment, differs. Some believe they are in a stable area and are happy to make their processes more fixed while others seek to be highly agile.

Finally, the *investment* dimension indicates the level of immediate versus long-term gain being sought. In business, this generally indicates whether returns are being reinvested or returned to shareholders. In the noncommercial sector, this means increasing the long-term capability of the organization or delivering greater productivity, customer service to the stakeholders, or reducing the budget.

Each of the five dimensions should be mapped onto the framework shown in Figure 3.4. Two examples are shown in Figure 3.5 and Figure 3.6. The first is an example typical of a research and development (R&D) start-up that is willing to invest a great deal in the business, strongly focused on growth, and highly agile in response to a developing market, but with a low level of organizational complexity. The second example is a typical example of a mature complex company that is seeking to maximize return to investors and regards itself as reactive to market changes rather than shaping them.

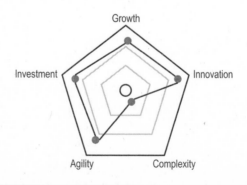

Figure 3.5   A Research and Development Start-up

Figure 3.6 A Mature Business

Leveraging an understanding of the organizational objectives, a model should be designed to govern information and supervise the internal information economy to achieve the best possible business outcome consistent with the strategic objectives of the enterprise. The following examples illustrate how the five dimensions align to different types of organization:

- *Growth.* The business that is focused on growth through acquisition, or organic increases in products and customers, should have a very strong emphasis on consistency of its information models and metadata to ease the integration of new customer groups, staff, products, and other data sets.

- *Innovation.* The CDO of an innovative organization will spend a lot of time ensuring that the collaborative metadata is well understood and properly used across all information stores, including structured databases and unstructured document repositories. The firm that is seeking to differentiate through innovation will try to maximize its business talent pool by creating a culture of collaboration across the business that is not dependent on hierarchy. In a meritocracy, business leaders must be prepared to promote initiatives that they find neither intuitive nor comfortable but that are thoroughly examined through modeling and peer review.

- *Complexity.* The organization that is trying to minimize its complexity should make good use of Small Worlds measures (discussed in Chapter 5) that are being constantly monitored by the CDO. Conversely, the businesses that recognize they are inherently complex need to understand the boundaries of information complexity and manage the models, metrics, and metadata closely to avoid the introduction of chaotic influences.

- *Agility.* The government enterprise that is seeking to maximize its stakeholder (public) service will often seek to use information to empower individual line service staff to make the right decision for their direct client while at the same time monitoring compliance with government policy and good budgetary discipline. Similarly, the commercial enterprise seeking to respond quickly to the market will distribute control of information and closely follow its development through centralized functions.

- *Investment.* The company that is reducing investment (usually to maximize cash flow) is likely to put a high priority on discipline and will not foster innovation at the frontline. After all, the main obstacle to maximizing cash is its diversion to new initiatives. This type of organization should usually use information most effectively to drive centralized control by a small number of business executives.

REPACKAGING OF INFORMATION

Given that information is a major asset of every organization, it makes sense for the board to be constantly thinking about the best way to extract value from the asset on behalf of the stakeholders (for example, the shareholders, or citizens, in the case of government enterprises). When information is considered only in terms of business processes, managers think only in terms of business process reengineering in its various guises. When information becomes an asset in its own right, with depreciation and organizational context, it becomes possible to think more radically about the theoretical application of the information in different ways.

For instance, if a business unit has a large customer base with regular interactions, it makes sense to look at how that customer data is leveraged by the enterprise as a whole. If the integration is minimal, as is often the case with many conglomerates, the value of the customer database could be considered in isolation and consideration given to redeploying or even selling it off as an asset to a third party who can achieve a higher rate of return on the asset.

When such sales are raised, concerns about customer relationships and privacy are often voiced. After all, information is often an asset with shared ownership. The ownership of any piece of information belongs to both the organization that holds custody of the content and to the stakeholders in the information such as the individual customer and their relations.

Every organization needs to be careful to meet all of its legal, moral, and assumed obligations; however, these can often be met in a variety of ways, and some of these ways might add greater value to the customers who could be frustrated by the limited scope of their relationship with the organization. For instance, a business that has a low financial return but regular customer contact could be of greater value when sold to another organization that can provide a greater level of service, and hence return, but needs an initial reason to develop a customer relationship.

Regardless of the mechanism, the process of information governance should put the information asset into stark relief treating it like any other capital that requires constant investment and maintenance and ties up shareholder funds.

LIFE CYCLE

Although information technology enables the quantity of information to grow, information is not part of the computer. Given that it is the key point of differentiation for almost every enterprise, the question thus becomes why so many businesses don't treat it as a key enterprise asset and dedicate the senior resources that it deserves. This is a matter of history and experience of the current generation of senior executives. The good news is that a new wave of executives is coming through the ranks who are leveraging information in new, innovative, and highly profitable ways.

The CDO has the responsibility to understand, explain, and govern the entire information life cycle. The role should provide the techniques to leverage information inside the enterprise and to turn it into the balance sheet asset that it deserves to be. This is not the role of the technology department on its own and the practitioners are just as likely to be part of finance, risk, merchandising, or any other skilled part of the business that uses complex information in its day-to-day activities.

There is a familiar refrain that the role of technology teams is to get closer to the business, to speak the language of the business, and to translate the complex world of computing. In the area of information, the CDO needs to make the argument that information is so complex that it is not appropriate to translate it into the language of an individual business, but rather it is time for every business to speak the language of information.

There is barely an executive of a major organization today who doesn't express frustration at the poor track record of information technology projects. What's promised is typically late, has much less functionality than was promised, and runs significantly over budget. Given that this is true across the globe, it may be time to stop sacking the technology team and to look inward to at least understand the issues.

When systems fail to live up to the early promises, it is seldom the case that the users are complaining about the colors of the boxes on their screen. While easy-to-use interfaces are important, they aren't the main measure of success. Broadly, the perception of success most closely correlates to the quality of the information contained in the system. Users will embrace a system with great and highly relevant data but will ignore easy-to-use systems with poor quality content or are irrelevant to their business needs.

In fact, there is a life cycle for systems related to information that is illustrated in four stages in Figure 3.7. In stage 1, when a system is first built, it is likely to have been well designed for user input, but more important, its content is highly relevant to the business of the enterprise. Almost inevitably, organizations change, and over time the content of the system is less relevant (stage 2). The usability of the system inevitably falls, ultimately leading to the point where it is irrelevant and hence virtually unusable (stage 3). The correct next action is to make the content more relevant and this will inevitably lead to a much better user experience through stage 4 and justifies investment for further improvement.

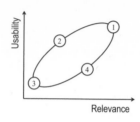

Figure 3.7   Usability to Relevance

There are some common mistakes that businesses make. When the user experience starts to fall, system owners focus on the usability axis because that is how the problem is described by the users. As if by gravity, no matter how much investment is made on the y-axis, without an investment in the x-axis, the usability falls as fast as improvements are made.

The other change that occurs all too often is that good systems are replaced for the want of a little more information that would make them highly relevant. When a new system is demonstrated, typically the user interface is combined with dramatically usable information. If the same information was available inside the existing system, the question needs to be asked whether it should be replaced.

Often, constant staff turnover is another cause of early system replacement. New data is needed within a given system and it is deemed too hard to make the change. There is no corporate memory of the data structures. The model is undocumented, the language of the system is outdated.

Today, systems are increasingly taking hundreds of staff several years to develop or even implement. With such a massive cost, the life of such systems can no longer be limited to five to ten years; rather they need to be capable of living for twenty or thirty years. If this challenge is to be met, the underlying information architectures need to be much more carefully considered.

Similarly, information challenges have often been tackled as an afterthought to system development. Hence the evolution of data warehousing, enterprise content management, and other information management solutions. All of these are a critical part of the information landscape, but they need to be integrated with the operational processes of the business rather than sit at the end of the food chain.

NOTES

1. J. B. Daley (2004), "Do You Really Know Who Your Customers Are? An Interview with Shep Parke of Accenture," *The Siebel Observer.*

2. R. Hillard and L. Na (2006), "Economic Value of Data for Financial Services Organizations," The Local and Global in Knowledge Management, Australian Conference for Knowledge Management and Intelligent Decision Support, December 5–6, 2005.

Chapter 4

Describing Structured Data

Before continuing on a journey through information management, it is important to have a common understanding of how information and data can be described in a structured way. Even unstructured data, such as documents, contains or relates to some form of structured data, such as the fields in a database.

Apart from truly random data sets, which have some limited value, every data set or document has relationships. For example, these relationships could exist between database fields, through a structure within a document, or as assumed associations between Web pages through keywords.

NETWORKS AND GRAPHS

There is, however, a very useful mathematical tool called graph theory that can be applied to gain a much deeper understanding of data. Graph theory describes networks of nodes. Network theory is formally called graph theory in mathematics; so for the balance of this chapter, consider the words *network* and *graph* to be synonymous.

Each node in the graph is called a vertex. The connections between vertices are called edges. We aren't talking about any other form of physical networking. Rather, we are discussing network theory in the abstract and applying theory from our mathematical colleagues to the newer science of information management, and specifically data modeling. The rules of data modeling are often lost in the detail of the individual business problem, so it is very useful to have some tools to help abstract the problem. Hence, each vertex corresponds to a data entity and each edge corresponds to a relationship between entities.

When we look at any organization of people, machines, or processes, we consider them not in isolation but as part of a connected whole. The factory fills the sales team's orders; the maintenance department services the customer warranty issues; and so on. Typically, we can draw this out as interconnected people, processes, and capabilities.

One of the simplest forms of a graph is a tree. The definition of a tree graph is one in which every node is connected to others by at most one path. This means that there are no complex interrelationships. Because there is only one path between

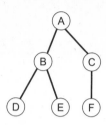

Figure 4.1   Tree Graph

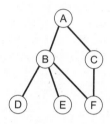

Figure 4.2   Not a Tree Graph

any two vertices, Figure 4.1 is a tree graph, whereas Figure 4.2 is not because there are multiple paths between vertices (for example, A-B-F and A-C-F).

In information science, the best known use of the tree graph is the Dewey Decimal Classification library filing system. Every book is filed using a decimal number (for example, 432.391). The highest level of division or class is:

000—Generalities
100—Philosophy and Psychology
200—Religion
300—Social Science
400—Language
500—Natural Science and Mathematics
600—Technology and Applied Sciences
700—Arts
800—Literature
900—Geography and History

Within each of these divisions are a further ten divisions. For instance, 500 (Natural Science and Mathematics) is further divided into:

We keep on dividing further, for instance Arithmetic is 513. The topic is further refined by adding decimal numbers.

Given that the most simple filing systems imply relationships (e.g., Arithmetic, 513, is a topic within Mathematics, 510), there is not much scope to support complex multipath relationships.

The first generation of data management software generally used these hierarchical structures. Not surprisingly, the first method used to represent data is also the simplest form of graph, separated by some three hundred years of mathematical experience. But computer and management science is catching up. We are now defining data management problems that can leverage many nineteenth-century graphing problems!

BRIEF INTRODUCTION TO GRAPHS

The history of graphs can be traced back to a question by the citizens of Konigsberg (now the Russian city of Kaliningrad). They posed the question: Is it possible to walk around our town using the seven bridges across the Pregel (later renamed Pregolya) river as shown in Figure 4.3?

In 1735, Leonard Euler presented his solution to the problem to the Russian Academy. He explained why crossing all seven bridges without crossing any bridge

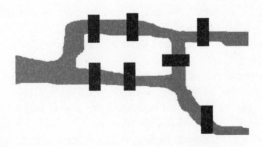

Figure 4.3   Seven Bridges of the Pregel River

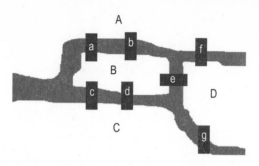

Figure 4.4   Seven Bridges with Labels

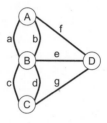

Figure 4.5   Euler's Abstraction

twice was impossible. While solving this problem, he laid the foundations for graph theory.

The first step in solving any problem is finding a way to codify or describe it in a systematic way. As in the case of the Konigsberg bridges, graph theory provides a way of describing real-world interfaces in a way that enables deep insight into the problem.

The first insight into this problem is that there are four areas that need to be passed through; we label them in Figure 4.4 as *A, B, C,* and *D.* The second insight is that there are seven paths between these areas that have been labeled *a, b, c, d, e, f,* and *g.*

Now Euler is able to remove all sense of geography from the problem. The areas become vertices and the paths become edges (see Figure 4.5).

Euler is now able to show that because there are an odd number of edges to more than one vertex, it is not possible to enter and exit by different bridges and still cross each bridge. Mathematicians quickly realized that the generalized terminology of the graph was perfect for abstracting many complex problems.

RELATIONAL MODELING

Relational modeling and normalization was originally defined by Edgar (Ted) Codd in a famous 1970 paper titled "A Relational Model of Data for Large Shared Data Banks."[1] Most students and practitioners know who Codd is and have some appreciation of the importance of his work. However, many people don't realize that Codd's work is both fundamental at a theoretical level and virtually unchallenged in its approach. Similarly, it is common for students to have a working knowledge of the principles of normalization, but when tested on the formal conventions, they struggle to define the underlying concepts.

Prior to relational modeling, information was almost always represented in a hierarchical structure with limited relationships being managed in computer code rather than described in the data itself. Not surprisingly, data was generally isolated to very specific applications with individual data banks being created to support each business function. Relational modeling opened up the data, abstracting it from the computer code that populated its content and enabling, almost for the first time, databases with content shared across many business applications.

Many people fall into the trap of believing that the relational model is only about relational databases. This is a shortsighted view and holds back the use of relational modeling as a logical tool for the enterprise. While the most effective way of storing structured relational data is using a relational database management system (RDBMS), it is not the only way, nor always appropriate. The RDBMS is nothing more than a rules-based file system.

Relational theory, on the other hand, is a rich way of analyzing and understanding the meaning of data and interpreting some of the business rule constraints. It is a special form of set theory. Generally it is not well understood, and we often treat the RDBMS as a list manager. Really the RDBMS is a server that allows us to manage files of data. Regardless of how we store the data (whether it be in an RDBMS, a spreadsheet, or in flat files), understanding the relational model is an important analysis step.

The brilliance of Codd's work is reflected in the fact that we all naturally normalize data in our heads whenever we see a list of names or numbers. Breaking content out into its fundamental elements and examining their relationships is a natural part of pattern analysis, something the human brain is specifically adapted to doing. Although we all do it, Codd has been able to codify the results in such a way that we now have a common language for our analysis, which in turn enables us to take an investigation into the meaning of any data much further.

Any analyst who has to look at any form of data, including statistics, marketing data sets, or tables of risk metrics, is able to do their job much more effectively if they understand the language of relational modeling. The skill will help them even if they never touch an RDBMS.

RELATIONAL CONCEPTS

The concept of relational data deserves to be revisited. A good example to use is a family tree. Consider one branch of the tree in which Andrew and Betty have three children, Charles, Dianne, and Esther. In the second branch of the family tree, Graham and Fran have two children, Harry and Ian (see Figure 4.6).

Because, in this example, each branch of the tree has one mother, one father, and either two or three children, when you identify one of the children it is possible to specify who their mother and father are. For example, if we specify Dianne, we know the father is Andrew and the mother is Betty. Similarly, if we specify Ian, we know the father is Graham and the mother is Fran. Logically, this means in conversation we could refer to Andrew uniquely as "Andrew," "Betty's partner," "Charles's father," "Dianne's father," or "Esther's father." All five descriptors uniquely define Andrew. In relational theory, we can say that the child defines the father or that the child is the determinant:

Child → Father

In this population of two branches of the family tree, the reverse is not true. If we identify either parent, we have identified a set of children but not any one individual. If we wanted to specify Charles, we can't say "child of Andrew," as this could be Charles, Dianne, or Esther. In relational theory, we say that the father does not determine the child.

Incidentally, while we could deduce Charles by saying "son of Andrew," using the relational analysis it can be shown that "son of Graham" does not uniquely define a child, as Graham and Fran have two sons, Harry and Ian.

The generic way of describing a relationship is between a determinant and an attribute, written as:

Determinant → Attribute

The relationship between the determinant and the attribute is known as the relationship cardinality. Cardinality indicates whether for every determinant there

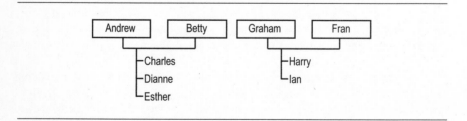

Figure 4.6 Two Branches of a Family Tree

is one or many attributes. A determinant/attribute relationship with a cardinality of one is known as a candidate key. A candidate key is normally more commonly known as the primary key.

There are some rules to how we manage data in a relational database. These rules are designed to avoid insertion, deletion, and update anomalies. To a lesser extent (at least today with reducing technology costs), they are also designed to reduce the volume of data being stored.

CARDINALITY AND ENTITY-RELATIONSHIP DIAGRAMS

The reason why all data cannot be represented in a single list is that some concepts exist more often in a data set than others. In the example of the family tree, there are more children (Charles, Dianne, Esther, Harry, and Ian) than parents (Andrew, Betty, Fran, and Graham). Using the terminology of determinants and attributes, there are usually (but not always) more attributes than determinants, although this doesn't have to be the case.

In this example, the child determines the father:

Child → Father

Another way of stating the relationship is to say each child in our defined population has one and only one father while each father can have more than one child. We draw this, as shown in Figure 4.7, using a "crow's foot" to indicate the entity that is the determinant.

For our data, we can also define whether a father has to have children and whether a child has to have a father. This can also be defined as a mandatory or optional relationship and is drawn in a relationship, as shown in Figure 4.8 and Figure 4.9 respectively, although this additional detail isn't always provided.

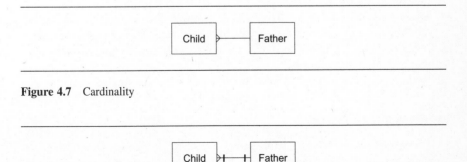

Figure 4.7 Cardinality

Figure 4.8 Mandatory Relationships

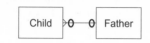

Figure 4.9 Optional Relationships

These figures are called Entity-Relationship (ER) diagrams. Each list of data is logically an entity and is drawn as a box. It is conventional to use the singular child rather than children when describing an entity. However, it does represent all children in the database. In this way, many lists are related to each other through their determinants and attributes.

NORMALIZATION

In order to interpret any data set, we need to decompose it to understand its constituent parts. The approach to this analysis is formally known as normalization. Normalization is the primary difference between a list and a relational data set. It converts a list of items into a set of relationships that can be interpreted. There are six levels of normalization in common use, which are described in the following sections.

1. *First Normal Form (1NF).* Providing an understanding of the subject by removing repeating groups.
2. *Second Normal Form (2NF).* Making it easy to see unique values by ensuring every element within the data set is dependent on the list determinants (called the primary key).
3. *Third Normal Form (3NF).* Extend the concept of 2NF by removing indirect (or transitive) dependencies.
4. *Boyce-Codd Normal Form (BCNF).* A stronger form of 3NF, which also requires that every determinant is part of the unique identifier or primary key.
5. *Fourth Normal Form (4NF).* Ensures that there is no misinterpretation by splitting out any multivalue fields.
6. *Fifth Normal Form (5NF).* Cleans up any multivalue constraints.

FIRST NORMAL FORM

In first normal form (1NF), repeating groups are to be eliminated. That means that any lists or multiple items that are imbedded within the same field (e.g., separated by commas) are recorded into separate rows. So the list of four rows becomes a list of six rows.

Consider the following list of car owners and their cars in Table 4.1.

Table 4.1   Original List

Name	Cars
Andrew	Volkswagen Golf, Ford Focus
Betty	Volkswagen Polo
Charles	Ford Focus
Deb	Mercury Sable, Volkswagen Golf

Table 4.2   1NF List

Name	Car
Andrew	Volkswagen Golf
Andrew	Ford Focus
Betty	Volkswagen Polo
Charles	Ford Focus
Deb	Mercury Sable
Deb	Volkswagen Golf

Table 4.3   1NF Table

Primary Key (PK)	Name	Car
11	Andrew	Volkswagen Golf
12	Andrew	Ford Focus
23	Betty	Volkswagen Polo
32	Charles	Ford Focus
44	Deb	Mercury Sable
41	Deb	Volkswagen Golf

While this is quite a common way to describe the data, it doesn't allow us much insight into the fundamental relationships. Consider the 1NF modified list in Table 4.2.

One of the technical requirements for every relational list or data set is the concept of a primary key. A primary key is a unique identifier for every row in any list or table. In Table 4.2, the most meaningful key we could create would be a numerical hybrid of the name and the car. In this example, we'll assign 1 to Andrew, 2 to Betty, 3 to Charles, and 4 to Deb. We'll also assign 1 to the Golf, 2 to the Focus, 3 to the Polo, and 4 to the Sable. The new list is shown in Table 4.3.

Of course, there is no reason why the primary key has to be numeric, but a hybrid based on the text of the name and text of the car is open to duplicates (such as two people with the name Andrew who are genuinely different people).

Table 4.3 is legal 1NF and meets the minimum technical requirements for relational data. It is also in the minimum form that is appropriate for a relational database.

SECOND NORMAL FORM

In second normal form (2NF), all attributes are dependent on the whole primary key. This has the effect of eliminating redundant data. Consider again Table 4.3, which is an example of 1NF; you should see that the same car is repeated against different individuals. We can see this analytically by looking at the primary key, which is dependent on both an individual and the car, meaning that an individual and a car can be repeated as long as the combination is unique.

To bring this table into 2NF, we have to split it out into a table of individuals and a table of cars (see Tables 4.4 and 4.5). We must also create a third list that relates the people and the cars together, as one car can be associated with more than one individual and vice versa (see Table 4.6).

We can illustrate the relationship of these three tables by using an ER diagram, as shown in Figure 4.10. As a reminder, each table is described as an entity and we show the relationships using the form described as part of the section on

Table 4.4   Individual Table

Primary Key (PK)	Name
1	Andrew
2	Betty
3	Charles
4	Deb

Table 4.5   Car Table

Primary Key (PK)	Car
1	Volkswagen Golf
2	Ford Focus
3	Volkswagen Polo
4	Mercury Sable

Table 4.6   Individual/Car Relationship Table

Primary Key	
Individual PK	Car PK
1	1
1	2
2	3
3	2
4	4
4	1

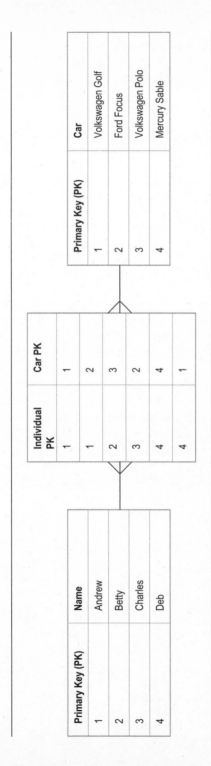

Figure 4.10 2NF Entity-Relationship Diagram

cardinality—that is, a line with a "crow's foot" at either end. It is important to remember that the "crow's foot" indicates that more than one row may exist in an indicated table for each individual row in the other table.

THIRD NORMAL FORM

In third normal form (3NF), we eliminate transitive dependencies. A transitive dependency is of the form:

$A \rightarrow B$ and $A \rightarrow C$

But in addition $B \rightarrow C$

In practice, this means identifying columns that, while dependent on the primary key, are logically independent. In 2NF, we split out redundant data that had been imbedded in the primary key (in this case, cars were being repeated). In 3NF, we look at the contents of the 2NF tables to see if there is any information that is common.

If we look carefully at the car table, we can see that it also describes manufacturer, which is actually being repeated. We can fix this by creating a separate manufacturer table, as shown in Table 4.7.

We also need to refer to the manufacturer table from within the car table (see Table 4.8).

This results in a new entity relationship diagram, as shown in Figure 4.11.

Many courses recommend that 3NF is as far as most practical database designers go; however, it is worth understanding fourth and fifth normal forms. Of course, as soon as they hear that, most students switch off. In fact, understanding higher level forms of normalization is essential if you are serious about using relational theory to better understand and test your subject matter. When you design your system, you may choose to still define the storage of your data in 3NF, but for your business

Table 4.7 Manufacturer Table

PK	Manufacturer
1	Volkswagen
2	Ford
3	Mercury

Table 4.8 3NF Car Table

PK	Car	Manufacturer
1	Golf	1
2	Focus	2
3	Polo	1
4	Sable	3

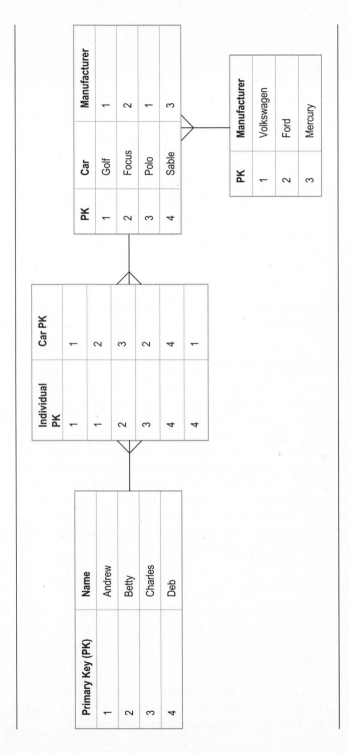

Figure 4.11 3NF Entity-Relationship Diagram

Table 4.9   First BCNF-Compliant Approach

Primary Key	
Surrogate Key	Manufacturer
1	Volkswagen
2	Ford
3	Mercury

Table 4.10   Second BCNF-Compliant Approach

Primary Key
Volkswagen
Ford
Mercury

understanding and supporting algorithms, you need to have an understanding of BCNF, 4NF, and even 5NF.

BOYCE-CODD NORMAL FORM

Boyce-Codd normal form (BCNF) is a variation on 3NF. You have to feel sorry for Ted Codd. He defined the levels of normalization as the basis of a whole new discipline, then shortly afterward decided that 3NF could do with some further tightening. Despite being the original designer of 3NF, his new definition was never accepted and is now known as Boyce-Codd Normal Form, or BCNF.

BCNF extends 3NF by requiring that any attribute that is capable of being used as a determinant also becomes part of the primary key. For example, in Table 4.7, a surrogate key was created for each manufacturer; however, in BCNF, if the name of the manufacturer is deemed to be unique, then it is also a determinant and needs to be part of the primary key. The BCNF-compliant version of the manufacturer table would be either Table 4.9 or Table 4.10.

FOURTH NORMAL FORM

Fourth normal form (4NF) fine-tunes the 3NF and BCNF models by removing any ambiguity about relationship tables by isolating any independent multiple relationships. A simple example might be to extend Figure 4.11 to include the manufacturer of the mobile phone owned by the individual (see Figure 4.12).

Since the association of phone is also a many-to-many, Figure 4.12 has simply included the relationship in the same resolving entity. This is a legal 3NF model; however, because the phone manufacturer is an independent determinant, it is not a legal 4NF model. The correct solution is shown in Figure 4.13.

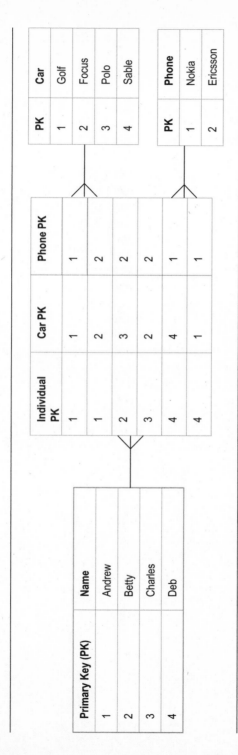

Primary Key (PK)	Name
1	Andrew
2	Betty
3	Charles
4	Deb

Individual PK	Car PK	Phone PK
1	1	1
1	2	2
2	3	2
3	2	2
4	4	1
4	1	1

PK	Car
1	Golf
2	Focus
3	Polo
4	Sable

PK	Phone
1	Nokia
2	Ericsson

Figure 4.12 Extended Car Model

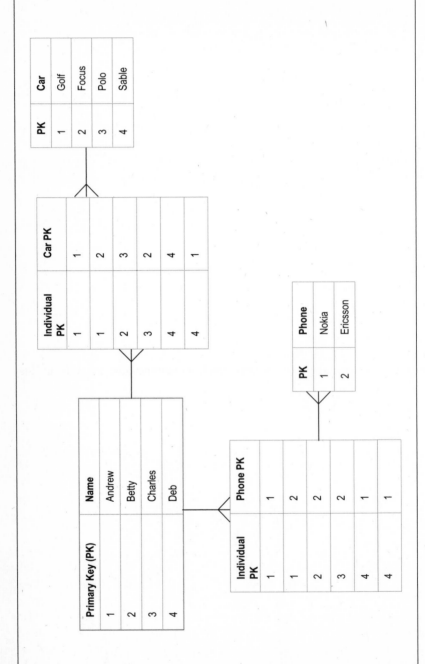

Figure 4.13 Correct 4NF Solution

FIFTH NORMAL FORM

Fifth normal form (5NF) is the same as 4NF except that any isolated relationships have to be brought back together. That means that if any tables have a dependency, then it is defined in a key. Figure 4.13 would be a legitimate 5NF solution if there is no constraint on which phones are used with which cars. If such a constraint did exist, the correct 5NF solution might look like Figure 4.14.

This is bad news for Andrew, who has bought an Ericsson phone but neither of his cars is permitted by this 5NF model to use it. Such a simple example is obvious and explains why manufacturers of in-car phone kits have moved to support connection to many different brands of phones. The value of 5NF models, though, is in exposing these business issues in situations that may be less evident.

IMPACT OF TIME AND DATE ON RELATIONAL MODELS

Relational theory is about gaining insight into the business rules that govern data. A close examination of the normalization rules shows that anything that defines a record is also regarded as part of a key. Time (such as the date and time that a transaction is processed) usually defines the record if only in terms of sequence. As such, time needs to be considered in terms of the rules of normalization and often needs to be part of a key.

Time is often a determinant in combination with another concept; for instance, date combined with employee number might determine how many hours they worked (worked hours being the attribute):

Employee Number+Date → Hours Worked

At the very least, time and date is often converted into derived information. For instance, date is often converted into day of the week or accounting period:

Date → Day of Week

Date → Accounting Period

Time is probably one of the most misused and miscoded concepts in databases today. Typically, a time stamp attribute is added to entities to represent concepts, such as when a product was purchased or when a transaction was posted.

It does not make sense, therefore, to treat time and date fields as simple free-form attributes. If they are determinants, they need to be managed as part of a master list or entity. Because time is one of the most complicated and important relationships in almost any network or system, it deserves to be an entity in its own right. This concept is discussed further in Chapter 12.

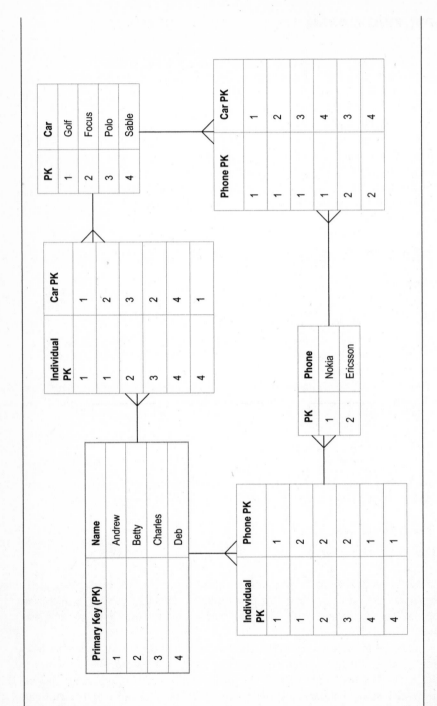

Figure 4.14 Potential 5NF Solution

APPLYING GRAPH THEORY TO DATA MODELS

Although Codd did a brilliant job of founding relational theory using a form of algebra, he introduced no theoretical anchor to analyze the wider structure of relationships of data models. It is not surprising, since in 1970 this was not a major priority, given that the concept of data being shared widely across the enterprise was new and largely untested.

The ER diagram has already been introduced in this chapter. As shown, there is a lot of information contained within individual relationships, and particularly across many relationships. From an ER diagram, you can determine the level of normalization. You can also deduce many business rules; for instance, Figure 4.15 implies that every customer has a relationship manager who also looks after one or more geographic areas.

As a new science, however, there is very little language in common use that allows practitioners to share deep insights about data models. Conversations, beyond the level of normalization, are generally limited to the subject of the model itself.

An alternative is to leverage the language of graph theory. Every entity is a vertex and each relationship is an edge, as shown in Figure 4.16.

The first thing we learn from graphs is that every node must be a minimum of one edge away from every other node. The implication of this is self-evident. Every

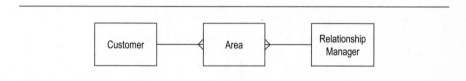

Figure 4.15   A Simple ER Diagram Can Describe a Lot

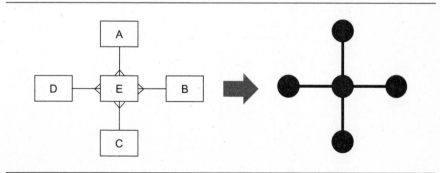

Figure 4.16   ER Diagram Represented as a Graph

entity is at least one relationship away from any other entity with which it is associated. In the unlikely event that there is no relationship possible between two entities, then they are an infinite number of edges apart.

DIRECTED GRAPHS

A directed graph or digraph is a set of directed relationships. Digraphs extend the concept of a graph to define pathways. The difference between an undirected graph and a directed graph is like the difference between two-way roads and one-way streets.

Consider the following problem of finding the shortest route between Bob and Jane's houses in Figure 4.17.

We can redraw this problem using a graph, as in Figure 4.18.

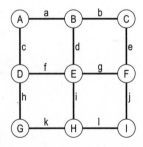

Figure 4.17   Bob and Jane's Houses

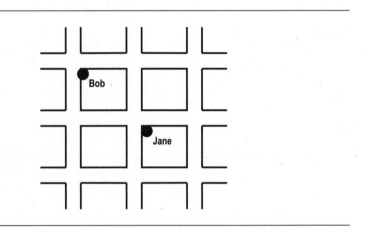

Figure 4.18   Graph Representation

Drawn as a graph, the problem becomes how to get from vertex *A* to vertex *E*. The two, equally short, solutions are paths *a-d* or *c-f*.

Now we introduce some one-way streets, which we draw as a directional graph or digraph. Examining Figure 4.19, the shortest pathway from *A* to *E* is now *a-b-e-j-l-i*.

Digraphs find many mathematical uses representing hierarchies such as social structures or biological food chains. They are equally useful for describing the one to many relationships between two entities.

Figure 4.20 shows how the cardinality of an entity relationship can be represented with a digraph. The direction of the flow between A and B (i.e., the direction of the graph) has a very specific meaning. For two entities to have a relationship, one must have an attribute that is a foreign key pointing to the primary key of the other.

Readers concerned about the direction of the digraph are reminded that A contains the determinant and B the attribute with the generally accepted notation being A→B.

NORMALIZED MODELS

We can use graph theory to help us understand how well normalized a data model is without needing to deeply examine the meaning of each relationship. A good

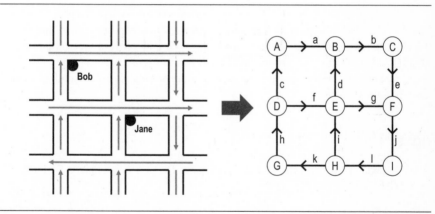

Figure 4.19   One-Way Streets Represented as a Digraph

Figure 4.20   ER Diagram Represented as a Digraph

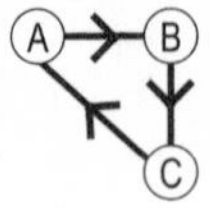

Figure 4.21   Circular Dependency

indication (although certainly not a requirement) that a data model meets the requirements of 3NF is if every relationship can be drawn in one of two directions (e.g., right and down or left and up). While this is a well-known principle, it is often hard to test. It is also hard to prove why it is the case.

Recall that in 3NF (the most common form of normalization), all redundant data imbedded in the primary key has been spit out and that columns not dependent on the primary key have been eliminated. The elimination of redundancy requires unambiguous relationships. Consider the following relationships:

A→B (that is, a particular row in table A defines a row in table B)
B→C
C→A

Because A→B and B→C, it can be determined that A→C. Since this means that A→C and C→A, there is ambiguity in the relationship between A and C and there is, therefore, redundancy in primary keys. Graphs prove a systematic way to identify any such circular dependency, as shown in Figure 4.21.

In Chapter 5, we will use graphs to gain a deeper insight into usability of data models in business.

NOTE

1. E. F. Codd (June 1970), "A Relational Model of Data for Large Shared Data Banks," *CACM* 13(6).

Chapter 5

Small Worlds Business Measure of Data

The massive growth in raw data volume through recent decades has created a new problem for the chief information officer (CIO): how to know whether the electronic content is stored in such a way that it is available and compelling for every stakeholder and potential user. Given the importance of the information asset, it is hard to believe that business executives have no way of determining whether it is being stored in a way that is readily accessible.

Information technology experts know that the accepted technique for storing structured data is in a relational database management system (RDBMS) using normalized relational modeling techniques, while unstructured content should be indexed using an enterprise taxonomy (a filing system or catalog). Business stakeholders, on the other hand, know that they need to have access to information but seldom have any understanding of the techniques used by the technologists or how they can strategically evaluate the quality of the data held by the enterprise.

As the wider economy has become focused on the generation and consumption of information, much of the economic value of any company or enterprise is tied up in its data. To have a critical business asset encoded in ways that are beyond the comprehension of the key executives of the business is an unacceptable risk and one that the Small Worlds measures, introduced in the following sections, helps to overcome.

SMALL WORLDS

You're sitting in an airport in Frankfurt and recognize the accent behind you. When you turn around, you realize that you went to school with the speaker. It's happened to us all, and we say, "What a small world."

In 1967, Stanley Milgram published a groundbreaking article in the popular magazine *Psychology Today* titled "The Small World Problem."[1] While the results were controversial, his initial work showed that most social chains connected one individual with any other in a small number of steps (popularly regarded as six steps, Milgram's research showed even closer relationships in the U.S. population that were the subject of his study). The Small Worlds network theory was formally born and it has continued to evolve. The theory shows that any network (be it technical, biological, or social) is stable only if there is a logarithmic relationship between the number of nodes and the number of steps needed to navigate between any two points.

A useful example to consider is the telephone network. Two neighbors calling each other might require two steps to complete a call (the caller connects to the nearest exchange, which then connects the call to the neighbor). By comparison, a call made between Sydney and New York may require only three or four steps to complete (the caller connects to a local exchange, then to an international exchange, then to an exchange local to the receiving party, and finally to the target of the call). The two transactions in this example demonstrate the extremes of telephony complexity. The first is the simplest that can be performed on the network, while the second is the most complex. Despite this, there is little difference in the number of network steps required.

This model holds true for programming languages. Most software development tools are designed to make it easy to navigate between code units (through the use of objects or subroutines). Physical storage technologies are designed to make it easy to request the retrieval of data regardless of whether it is adjacent or distributed over a substantial distance. The Internet is the ultimate example of a distributed system with a logarithmic relationship between distance and complexity.

The model also holds true for successful business models. For example, sales teams rely on internal communications to mirror the large accounts against which they are applied. Good organization hierarchies support communication from any obscure part of an enterprise to any other with only a few managers required to complete the contact.

The one example that consistently breaks this principle is the network of relationships in a data model that is used to link all of the context information described earlier. As we shall see in a moment, typical data models within a single function database require dozens of steps to join together even closely related concepts and hundreds or even thousands of steps to link across the enterprise in new ways.

MEASURING THE PROBLEM AND SOLUTION

The value of data is as much in its relationships as in its content. Described another way, the value is in the network of data relationships and while data exists on the computer network, its relationships are not necessarily appropriately networked.

Senior executives can direct technology staff to use appropriate data management techniques to improve the data network across the enterprise; however, it is difficult to promote good behavior without a mechanism to measure its adoption. While technical staff know they are being measured by their productivity, as measured by solving individual tasks, they know it is unlikely executives will ever examine the way they store data in data models.

Executives need a set of measures to ensure that new content is loaded onto the corporate network in a way that simplifies its application to new business functions rather than hindering new development. The metrics need to be a level above the concepts of normalization and general database management. Such a technique needs to simplify the data model to its constituent parts and require very little technical skill to apply.

ABSTRACTING INFORMATION AS A GRAPH

To give this discussion a solid foundation of theory, it is necessary to start with the concept of a graph as introduced in Chapter 4. As a reminder, in mathematics, a graph is a network of vertices (or nodes) connected by edges, thus forming a network like the example shown in Figure 5.1.

Many readers may still be confused by the term *graph*, as they will only know it as a visual representation of a set of numbers, such as shown in Figure 5.2. For

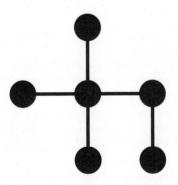

Figure 5.1   Example Graph

Figure 5.2   The "Other" Type of Graph

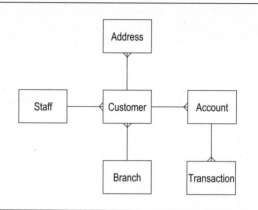

Figure 5.3   Example Entity-Relationship Diagram

this discussion, the term *graph* will be used in purely the mathematical sense, joining vertices by edges.

Information technology professionals would generally be comfortable with the representation of structured data as an Entity-Relationship (ER) diagram, such as the example shown in Figure 5.3.

The visualization of unstructured data requires a much more abstract thought process. Unstructured content refers to concepts of documents, Web pages, e-mails, and other information that is not in a fixed or mandated structure. Well-managed repositories of this content are indexed based upon a taxonomy. For instance, a bank might use a taxonomy that mandates indexing by staff member, branch, customer, account, and transaction. In which case, the taxonomy is also well represented by Figure 5.3.

In the case of both structured and unstructured data, it takes little imagination to see how Figure 5.1 is a good abstraction of Figure 5.3.

METRICS

A graph is described by its order (the number of vertices), size (the number of edges), vertex degree (the number of edges intersecting a given vertex), and geodesic distance (the length of the shortest path between a pair of vertices). The graph in Figure 5.1 has an order of 6 (the number of vertices) and size of 5 (the number of edges or links between the vertices).

Using these new terms (order, size, degree, and geodesic distance), executives should consider three key metrics: average degree, average geodesic distance, and maximum geodesic distance.

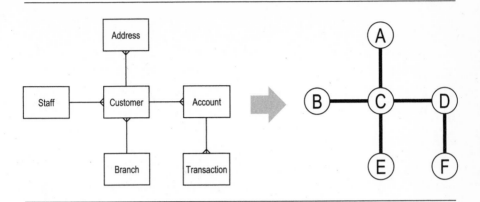

Figure 5.4 Example Graph with Labels

Table 5.1 Degree and Geodesic Distance (Separation)

1	2	3	4	5	6	7	8	9	10
Vertex	**Degree**			**A**	**B**	**C**	**D**	**E**	**F**
A	1		**A**		2	1	2	2	3
B	1		**B**	2		1	2	2	3
C	4		**C**	1	1		1	1	2
D	2		**D**	2	2	1		2	1
E	1		**E**	2	2	1	2		3
F	1		**F**	3	3	2	1	3	

To illustrate their use, we'll restate the ER diagram used previously and abstract it to a graph, labeling each node as shown in Figure 5.4.

Next, build a table to record the degree of each vertex and the geodesic distance between each pair of vertices. The format of such a table for our worked example is shown in Table 5.1.

Columns 1 and 2 record the vertex (node) of the graph and the number of edges (connections) attached to each. Columns 4 through 10 show the number of steps required to traverse the graph between any two vertices.

The *average degree* is calculated by averaging the second column in Table 5.1 (1, 1, 4, 2, 1, and 1) giving an average degree of 1.67.

The *maximum geodesic distance* is determined by looking at the right side of the table (columns 4 to 10) and finding the highest separation between any two vertices. In this case, the largest separation is between either A and F or B and F, both of which require three steps as the maximum geodesic distance.

The *average geodesic distance* is calculated by averaging the same separations examined when calculating maximum geodesic distance. The shaded cells should not be counted in either the numerator or the denominator. The simplest way to

Table 5.2 Separations Extracted for Averaging

4	5	6	7	8	9	10
	A	B	C	D	E	F
A		2	1	2	2	3
B			1	2	2	3
C				1	1	2
D					2	1
E						3
F						

perform the calculation is to average the cells extracted from Table 5.1 as shown in Table 5.2.

There are 15 cells identified in Table 5.2 with an average separation of 1.87.

INTERPRETING THE RESULTS

A final useful consideration to understand the nature of the information being held is the ratio of size (5) to order (6). If the ratio is <1, then (generally) more of the information is held in content. However, if the ratio is >1, then the majority of the information is about the relationships.

Like any benchmark, the key is to seek constant improvement. As a start, each critical database and repository in the enterprise should be assessed and any future developments (either modifications to existing systems or the addition of new databases) should result in all three measures being lowered.

For any database requiring human access (such as through a query or reporting tool), it is important to remember that a single query that requires more than four steps is beyond an average user. Anything requiring 10 or more steps is beyond anyone but a trained programmer prepared to invest substantial time in testing. That means the average geodesic distance should approach 4 and organizations should aim for a maximum geodesic distance of approximately 10. The average and maximum results of 1.87 and 3 in the example of the previous section indicate a tightly integrated data model seldom requiring more than one or two steps to answer a question.

Average degree reflects the options a user faces to navigate a database. Realistically, 3 or 4 direction options on average is manageable, but as the number approaches 10 nothing other than well-tested code can possibly manage the complexity. The result of 1.67 in the worked example of the previous section indicates that there are few alternative pathways and little likelihood of ambiguity.

These measures encourage good data management practice. Even systems that are not designed for direct human access on a daily basis should be measured in this way. Too often, core operational systems become an obstacle to data extraction and further business transformation.

NAVIGATING THE INFORMATION GRAPH

Most data models are used in support of business or other organizations. The entities represent stocks or stores of information within processes or the organization structure. In Figure 5.3, we show a direct relationship between a staff member and a customer (i.e., each customer is looked after by one and only one staff member). For the purposes of this exercise, it is not necessary for the reader to understand the nuances of data modeling, but for the purpose of completeness, each relationship (edge) includes an indication of quantity as shown in Figure 5.5 and described more fully in Chapter 4.

In the example of the staff to customer relationship, we can conclude that there is a close relationship between the staff member and the individual customer. But what if each staff member in the bank is responsible only for a limited range of products? In which case, a customer is likely to deal with more than one staff member. One product staff member deals with multiple customers and one customer deals with multiple product staff.

A technical rule of entity relationship modeling requires that a so-called many-to-many relationship is not possible and must be resolved as shown in Figure 5.6.

The reason for this requirement relates to the way a relationship is codified in a database table. The many end of the relationship can only record a key for one parent record (otherwise there would be many entries, which breaks the rules of normalization). In the simpler Figure 5.3 relationship between customer and staff, each customer record would record a staff key. When a customer can relate to more than one staff member, it is no longer possible to pick one staff key to insert in the record. The Customer Relationship entity in Figure 5.6 records pairs of staff and customer keys allowing any number of relationships to be created.

Importantly for the information graph analysis, where the staff and customer relationship in Figure 5.3 are directly connected (in other words, they are connected by just one link or edge), the more complicated relationship described in Figure 5.6 requires two steps and can be described as having a separation of 2. This fits our

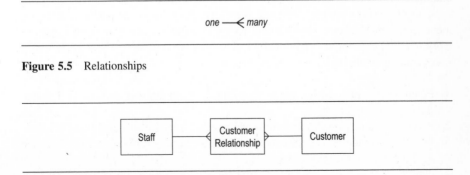

one ——< *many*

Figure 5.5 Relationships

Figure 5.6 Many-to-Many Relationship

real-world expectations—a customer who deals with only one staff member is going to feel closer to the bank than one who has to deal with an array of staff.

INFORMATION RELATIONSHIPS QUICKLY GET COMPLEX

Just as important as the business insight we gain from the analysis of business practices is the need to be able to retrieve information when we need it, in the form we need, and without layers of interpretation. Most business executives do not have the confidence to examine or even retrieve data themselves. That would be acceptable if an assistant was directly sourcing the information the executive needed, but the reality is usually very different and teams of middle management expend large amounts of their time trying to assemble data sets in the form requested. There are three major problems.

First, the complexity of assembling the data leads inevitably to error. Often, associations are stretched beyond statistically acceptable levels or the complexity of the information pathway results in wrong pathways being selected and incorrect associations being made. Second, the information that is provided is highly interpreted, which means that the underlying subtleties of the data are lost and, in turn, opportunities for further analysis are not realized. Third, the sheer volume of work created by information requests means that the lag between asking for and receiving critical metrics discourages logical follow-up questions. The process becomes more like programming ancient punch card mainframes than using twenty-first-century intuitive technology.

To understand why the complexity of the information multiplies so easily, consider a simplified example of a school. Each student may have one or more parents and siblings. The same student belongs to a year level and is enrolled in one or more subjects. Each year level is supported by a staff faculty and each subject is taught by one or more teachers. This example is already complex without needing to add real-world sophistication! Figure 5.7 provides a diagrammatic view of the data in the form of the ER diagram we described earlier.

Consider now a simple question: Which teachers should an individual parent meet on parent-teacher night? Without trying to write the query, the first step is to work out the paths between parent and teacher and we find that there are potentially four (without doubling back to the same entity). The paths are:

1. Parent → Family → Student → Year Level → Syllabus → Subject → Teacher Assignment → Teacher
2. Parent → Family → Student → Year Level → Year Level Faculty → Teacher
3. Parent → Family → Student → Enrollment → Subject → Teacher Assignment → Teacher
4. Parent → Family → Student → Enrollment → Subject → Syllabus → Year Level → Faculty → Teacher

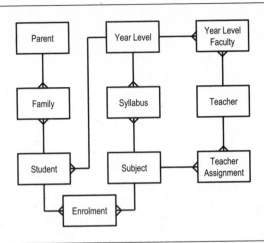

Figure 5.7　School ER Model

The problem that this data model faces is that while it is logically correct, there is a substantial separation between two core concepts (parent and teacher) and there is ambiguity in the information pathways.

While a good data modeler can look at the preceding list and point out that only pathway three is likely to be valid, there is nothing in the model that makes this true and it requires additional external knowledge. To know that pathway three is correct, the reader needs to know that the association of student to subject via enrolment provides a list of actual subjects attended and the teacher assignment is the closest available relationship of those subjects to the teacher.

Worse, the number of steps involved in navigating the pathways between parent and teacher mean that it is impossible to predict what relationships will be produced and even harder to test their validity. The ER data model in Figure 5.7 describes an everyday business problem, and yet even this simple example has four different pathways between two key entities.

To understand the problem better, it is useful to now analyze Figure 5.7 using the principles and metrics established earlier. First, abstract the model into a graph as shown in Figure 5.8.

The degree and geodesic distance table is shown in Table 5.3.

The average degree of this model is 2.2, indicating that there are usually multiple pathways to choose from (and hence users of this model will have to deal with ambiguity).

The maximum geodesic distance is five, which, while not excessive in comparison to many real-world data models, is large for a simple business problem (like associating students, teachers, and parents). One way to think of it is in terms that Stanley Milgram defined social separation. Globally, Milgram's research showed

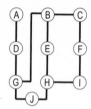

Figure 5.8 Abstracted School Model

Table 5.3 Degree and Geodesic Distance Table

Vertex	Degree			A	B	C	D	E	F	G	H	I	J
A	1		A		3	4	1	4	5	2	4	5	3
B	3		B	3		1	2	1	2	1	2	3	2
C	2		C	4	1		3	2	1	2	3	2	4
D	2		D	1	2	3		3	4	1	3	4	2
E	2		E	4	1	2	3		3	2	1	2	2
F	2		F	5	2	1	4	3		3	2	1	3
G	3		G	2	1	2	1	2	3		2	3	1
H	3		H	4	2	3	3	1	2	2		1	1
I	2		I	5	3	2	4	2	1	3	1		2
J	2		J	3	2	4	2	2	3	1	1	2	

that there were seldom more than six degrees of separation between humans throughout the world. It would be expected to be far less within a single school community!

The average geodesic distance is 2.4, which indicates that most associations can be made with between two and three steps. While the maximum geodesic distance is clearly a problem, the average geodesic distance is, in this case, within acceptable bounds as defined earlier.

There are many ways that expert modeling can solve the problems identified in this example, some of which will be discussed in Chapter 10. By providing simple metrics as outlined, the problem is highlighted and the technical experts can be engaged. Further, with these metrics as a guide, the solution provided by the expert team can be evaluated by the business stakeholders without resorting to a technical understanding of modeling principles.

USING THE TECHNIQUE

There are many ways this technique can be immediately applied with dramatic management impact. One of the most obvious builds on the concept of information sharing highlighted in Chapter 1. In the information economy, the value of conglomerates is arguably only achieved when there is a tight coupling of information. Banks that don't share customer information are unable to realize any cross-sell advantage over their more specialized competitors, although they remain at an agility disadvantage.

Analysts can illustrate the problem and opportunity by mapping the Small World metrics around just key data items, such as customer, product, and geography. This analysis should go across business unit divisions and provide metrics about showing the number of steps required to link customer data in one division with product data in another business unit. Such an approach is particularly useful when considering mergers, acquisitions, and the sale of business units. Buyers of businesses can use this approach to get a real insight into the usability of the data, which is claimed to be held within the company's databases. Sellers can map the relationships across multiple dataset to determine where the most logical point of separation would be within a conglomerate.

Ultimately, though, leaders should be using Small Worlds measures to achieve better information sharing as described in Chapter 1. Where the sharing of infrastructure was, in earlier decades, a major consideration in the development of large conglomerates, information is now the major opportunity for leverage by larger businesses and even government entities. If islands of data appear when developing Small Worlds graphs of data across the enterprise, then clearly there is little information sharing occurring, and a strong argument for either radical change or the sale of either the business or, at the very least, the isolated data.

NOTE

1. S. Milgram (1967), "The Small-World Problem," *Psychology Today* 1: 60–67.

Chapter 6

Measuring the Quantity of Information

The science of information management continues to evolve, and most practitioners are working based on experience rather than hard metrics, making it difficult to solve problems that seem to consistently afflict enterprises the world over. In this situation, it is very important to discover if techniques sought from other branches of science can be applied to information management.

Long before computers were invented, physicists were working on complex systems that had many states through the study of thermodynamics. Each state could be thought of as being equivalent to coded information.

As with the application of graph theory to the subject, understanding the quantity of information in the way that physics analyses complex systems is of great value. With clear numeric measures on quantity, it becomes possible to analyze how much information is being applied to a given business objective and whether there is unused potential hidden in databases, documents, and spreadsheets.

A measure of quantity is particularly important in the context of the information economy, which must trade in data. In any transaction, currency is only meaningful if it is tied, in some way, to a quantity.

DEFINITION OF INFORMATION

There are many definitions of information, which in itself suggests that information management professionals have a challenge establishing the principles consistently in business. One of the more succinct definitions has been suggested by Robert M Losee:[1]

> Information is produced by all processes and it is the values of characteristics in the processes' output that are information.

This definition captures the concept that information results from events or processes, and just as important, it is the number of unique states of each output (the values) that correspond to information. For instance, a coin produces two states or values when tossed: heads or tails.

The definition implies values based on the context of the information. There was a time when it was argued that, in some disciplines, the context of information was irrelevant. For instance, a communications engineer was only interested in transmitting as many binary bits as physically possible over a wire or given radio spectrum. Twenty-first-century engineers know that the context of the information being transmitted provides enormous opportunities for data compression and that this increases the volume of information that can be transmitted. For instance, in many contexts yes, Y, and true are synonyms, and hence represent one piece of unique information with just two potential states or values.

A clever aspect of Losee's definition is that it ties information to process. He goes on to recognize that processes are simply algorithms of varying levels of complexity. Once again, information is more closely tied to algorithms than it is to static metrics. Said differently, information is dynamic.

THERMAL ENTROPY

Another discipline that examines dynamic systems is thermodynamics. Thermodynamics is the study of physical systems (such as gasses) at the macroscopic level under different conditions of pressure and temperature. The most fundamental approach to thermodynamics is statistical thermodynamics, which recognizes the existence of individual particles and applies probabilities across the population.

The number of degrees of freedom or states that can be applied to a given volume of a gas corresponds to the amount of information that is needed to fully describe the system. If there were two molecules of gas in a container with four possible positions that each molecule is permitted to be, as shown in Figure 6.1, then the system has a total of eight states. Each particle can be in any one of four

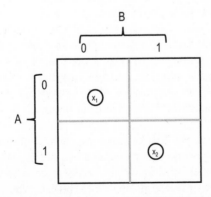

Figure 6.1 Simple Gas in Small Box

locations independent of the other and there are two particles; therefore, there are two times four possible states.

The analogy to the management of information is compelling. By arbitrarily using the two particles to encode each of the four boxes, a number between one and eight (or zero and seven) could be defined. For the purpose of the example, it does not matter what coding system is used.

Physicists have sought to generalize the behavior of the collection of particles of the gas and created the concept of entropy to describe the energy potential of a given volume. Entropy is defined to be the degree of freedom and the number of states that can be represented in a given system. The most fundamental definition of entropy, in statistical thermodynamics, is:

$$k_B \ln \Omega$$

Where k_B is Boltzmann's constant ($1.38066 \times 10{-}23 \, \mathrm{J\,K^{-1}}$) and Ω represents the number of individual states the system can be in (for a gas, this can be a very large number!). Thermodynamic entropy is expressed in terms of Joules of energy for every degree Kelvin of the system, which is simply a convenience introduced by the Boltzmann constant and the use of the natural logarithm.

For readers who don't recall their high school physics, a Joule is a measure of energy, and by measuring the number of Joules a quantity of gas is capable of storing at a given temperature, it is effectively a measure of energy capacity. The important concept is that the number indicating energy capacity is directly proportional to the number of states, making entropy effectively a measure of the amount of information that a gas could theoretically encode.

INFORMATION ENTROPY

Claude Shannon (1916–2001) was a distinguished electrical engineer and mathematician who established many groundbreaking principles in the areas of Boolean logic, electrical transmission of data, and information theory. Today, Shannon is regarded by many as the father of information theory, and a paper he wrote in 1948 is potentially its conception. "A Mathematical Theory of Communication"[2] was written before magnetic computer storage had been invented and was most concerned with the abstract transmission of information, yet the insight he provided in the paper is as groundbreaking and relevant today as it was when it was first written.

Shannon's paper was the first to apply the concept of entropy to information, on the basis that Joules per degree of temperature (energy potential) was analogous to the information potential of messages and storage devices. Thermal entropy measures the amount of energy that can be absorbed, while information entropy measures that amount of information that can be encoded. Shannon chose to use the word bit to define information entropy when analyzing binary digital capacity (i.e., two states) and decimal digits when analyzing devices with 10 states. Given the wider adoption of the bit, representing the smallest numerical unit possible and as the basis of digital computer storage (zero or one), it is sensible to adopt the bit as the standard measure of information entropy.

It is important to note that the information entropy use of the unit bit is slightly different to the storage use of the same word. Entropy means capacity and does not need to be measured in integers. For example, it makes sense to talk about 0.5 bits of information entropy. In contrast, when describing computer storage, each bit must be whole and is only meaningful as an integer.

Starting from first principles of information entropy, if an abstract device can represent one bit (i.e., a zero or a one) and we have no knowledge of the content of that bit, then we define the Shannon entropy or information entropy to be one bit. An example of such a device would be a coin that can be placed with either the head or tail side up.

In his paper, Shannon explains that a device that can store H bits has 2^H possible settings, if we use N to represent the number of settings, then $N = 2^H$. This makes sense mathematically and logically. One device (e.g., a single coin) can store two states (heads or tails). A device consisting of two coins can store two states on each coin, which means combined it is storing two times two or 2^2 states. A device consisting of three coins stores two states (heads or tails) on each coin and in combination represents two times two times two or 2^3 different states.

Conversely, if we know a device has N settings, then the number of bits can be calculated by $H = log_2N$. As a reminder, the log function is simply the inverse of raising a number to a power. If $N = 2^H$, then $H = log_2N$.

Table 6.1 enumerates this relationship for a number of important values of N and H. There is, of course, no reason why N has to be a power of 2. Since computers are fundamentally chains of binary devices joined together, they most effectively model or represent real-world systems that are also powers of 2. However, the reality is that a real-world system can have any number of states. For example, most dice have six sides or states, and when combined have six to the power of the number of dice.

Table 6.1 Relationship of States to Bits

N (states)	H (bits) $= log_2N$
2	1
4	2
8	3
16	4
32	5
64	6
128	7
256	8

Many readers with some background in computer science will recognize the last result for N and H of 256 and 8, respectively, representing the number of states that can be represented by a computer byte.

Shannon went on to describe the quantity H as the information entropy, and, as already described, generalized that if the base 2 was used, then the units of information entropy were bits. The entropy of a device with N states and for which we have no knowledge of the content (which will be explained shortly) is:

$$H = log_2 N$$

Since entropy represents what we don't know about a given system, we need to apply any knowledge that we do have. For instance, in most situations we have some knowledge of what a particular computing device is going to be used for, and in particular what a given byte is going to be used for. So while an eight bit byte has 256 states, often we are simply storing one of 26 alphabetic characters, so the real entropy is less than the idealized situation we identified earlier. In that case, the entropy would be $log_2 26$, or 4.7 bits.

The insight this provides us is that while the computer storage used to hold the alphabetic character is eight bits long, the actual information entropy is more than 40 percent less at 4.7 bits. There is less decision-making information than the raw data storage might suggest.

Shannon went further and recognized that not every state is of equal probability. For example, in the English language the letter e is far more prevalent than the letter z. Shannon's generalized entropy equation is:

$$H = -\sum_{i=1}^{n} p(x_i) log_2 p(x_i)$$

Where $p(x_i)$ is the probability that the device will be in a particular state. So, for a device holding one letter as part of an English word, the probability table is as follows (see Table 6.2).

Using these frequency-based probabilities, the entropy of an individual byte used to represent a single letter in the English language drops farther, to 4.18 bits. Again, the more we analyze the content, the less actual information is there. So while the computer storage for these letters is eight bits, the real usable information is nearly 50 percent less.

ENTROPY VERSUS STORAGE

One important application of information entropy is in the calculation of theoretical compression ratios for computer storage. In the case of a system containing eight bits (one byte) used to store an alphabetical character, the entropy is 4.18 bits, as described in the preceding section. That means that the ideal compression algorithm can achieve up to a compression rate of 48 percent, but not more:

Table 6.2 Frequency of Letters in English

A	8.17%
B	1.49%
C	2.78%
D	4.25%
E	12.70%
F	2.23%
G	2.02%
H	6.09%
I	6.97%
J	0.15%
K	0.77%
L	4.03%
M	2.41%
N	6.75%
O	7.51%
P	1.93%
Q	0.10%
R	5.99%
S	6.32%
T	9.06%
U	2.76%
V	0.98%
W	2.36%
X	0.15%
Y	1.97%
Z	0.07%

$$1 - \frac{4.18}{8}$$

It is important to note these ratios only apply to lossless compression—this is where content is reduced in size without compromise to the content. So-called lossy compression is often used for audio and video applications where a small compromise to the content can dramatically reduce its size.

There is a problem, however. In order to code a letter in an average of 4.18 bits (or even five bits for ease of programming), both writer and reader must have an agreed algorithm. It is clearly inefficient to describe this algorithm uniquely each time. Hence, common coding needs to be defined in a common algorithm dictionary, providing data to help us interpret the data: metadata.

Once again, there is a direct relationship between information and algorithms with an interpretive algorithm being needed to create the content and then to interpret it. The algorithm itself must also have a minimum size, although it can be reused by the author and reader for each instance of the same type of information.

More important than understanding potential savings in infrastructure, entropy provides insight into the real amount of information that is available to make decisions. Consider two retail shops (A and B). Both have an inventory of 100 items, and without further knowledge of their businesses, you know that the information entropy associated with the product in a single sale is $log_2 100$, or 6.64. Now, let's add the information that in store A, all 100 stock items sell at an approximately even rate, while in store B they have one line, which accounts for 40 percent of all sales, and five lines, which together account for 80 percent of all sales.

Shop A

Product	Probability
1 to 100	1%

Shop B

Product	Probability
1	40%
2 to 5	10%
6 to 100	$\frac{0.2}{95}$ or 0.21%

For shop A, the information entropy can be calculated using either method, giving the same result of 6.64 bits.

$$log_2 100 \; or \; -\sum_1^{100} \frac{1}{100} log_2 \frac{1}{100}$$

For shop B, however, only the second method can be used because the probabilities are not equal. Applying the information entropy gives a much lower result for shop B of 3.64.

$$-\left(0.4 log_2 0.4 + \sum_2^5 0.1 log_2 0.1 + \sum_6^{100} \frac{0.2}{95} log_2 \frac{0.2}{95} \right) = 3.64$$

What this means is that there is more information potential or content in shop A, where there is no prior knowledge of which product is most likely to be sold, than in shop B, where there is a heavy bias toward leading items.

As a final illustrative example, consider the storage of the words *YES* and *NO* in a field. In most cases, they are abbreviated to *Y* and *N* and stored in eight bits of computer storage, although some systems choose to spell them out in full and use 24 bits. The entropy, however, is not related to the storage but rather the number of permitted values. If the field is distributed 50 percent as *YES* and 50 percent as *NO*, then the entropy is:

$$-\sum_{1}^{2}0.5\,log_2\,0.5 = 1\;bit$$

Even more dramatic is the case where the flag is almost always *YES*. For instance, the field could be associated with a list of medical patients where the field indicates whether they are a foreign national. Consider the case where 95 percent of the entries are *NO*; then the entropy becomes:

$$-(0.95\,log_2\,0.95 + 0.05\,log_2\,0.05) = 0.3\;bits$$

Again, we are surprised when we compare the original eight bits that a Boolean (Yes/No) flag is allocated in a computer system with the usable data. In this very common and realistic example, we find that the usable data that can be applied to decision making is in fact only 0.3 bits or more than 96 percent smaller than the raw data storage capacity that is used to represent it!

ENTERPRISE INFORMATION ENTROPY

Organizations generate massive amounts of data in a variety of systems and business processes. Although many business processes are automated, there has been a focus on digitizing paper-based processes, making them faster and more flexible. In doing this type of automation, executives have seldom given more than a passing thought to the information that results from these business activities. This is the information asset.

To develop an effective information strategy to maximize the return on this important asset, it is necessary to first understand how much information exists in a meaningful unit of quantity. This can be done for any organization using the concept of information entropy, some simple steps, and some reasonable estimates. The estimates can be improved over time making the enterprise information entropy baseline increasingly accurate and useful.

The first step is to decide on a reasonable reporting period against which the quantity of information is measured. While stocks, as previously described, remain static, flows need to be measured within a particular time period. For many businesses, monthly reporting periods are the most meaningful. The period picked is a numerical convenience and ultimately doesn't matter as long as it is consistently applied to all information entropy measurements.

Reporting Period:	Monthly

The second step is to estimate how many distinct processes exist for the enterprise. This is initially a daunting task; however, most organizations will have undertaken regulatory and other compliance-related audits of key business processes that form the foundation of such an analysis. Start by listing the key value-creating processes for the enterprise.

Approximate number of processes:	50

Next, identify a small number (perhaps two or three) that are particularly critical and nominate them for a detailed (sample) analysis.

Process
Purchase new stock
Customer sale
Replenish stock

For each of the identified processes, now record the steps involved. Often this will already exist in some form. It's important to remember that this analysis is not a business process analysis; rather, it is just attempting to gain an understanding of the information embedded in the process. For the purpose of this exercise, the analysis is greatly simplified.

Process:	Purchase new stock
#	Step
1	Generate purchase order
2	Confirm receipt date
3	Record receipt

For each step, it is necessary to work out how many instances occur per reporting period (as identified earlier). In our working example, consider whether orders are generated by store or centrally and how many supplier orders are raised. In each case, we are interested in an approximate average.

Process:		Purchase new stock	
#	Step	Instances/Month	Notes
1	Generate purchase order	25,000	Central ordering of 1,000 items with one record per store (50)
2	Receive stock in store	50,000	Received in store (×50) on average in 2 batches
3	Position on shop floor	100,000	Each batch is distributed twice

For each step, it is now necessary to determine how many variables exist and the number of potential values they could hold. Keeping the example simple:

Process:	Purchase new stock	Step:	Generate purchase order
Variable	Allowable Values	Entropy (log_2)	Notes
Store	50	5.6	
Supplier	100	6.6	Number of registered suppliers
Quantity	Average 20	4.3	Simplified calculation
Stock item	2,000	11.0	Total range carried
Total instance entropy		**27.5**	
Process step entropy per month		**687,500**	Instance × 25,000 per month

We now know that the generate purchase order step in the purchase new stock process generates 687,500 bits of information per month. This calculation needs to be repeated for receive stock in store and position on shop floor. For the purposes of illustration, assume that the latter two process steps both generate one million bits per month.

Process:		Purchase new stock	
#	Step	Entropy per Month	Notes
1	Generate purchase order	687,500	Calculated above
2	Receive stock in store	1,000,000	Estimated
3	Position on shop floor	1,000,000	Estimated
Process entropy per month		**2,687,500**	

Then, repeat the calculation for each of the other sample processes (customer sale and replenish stock). For the purpose of this example, assume that both generate 3 million bits per month.

Process	Entropy per Month	Notes
Purchase new stock	2,687,500	
Customer sale	3,000,000	Estimated
Replenish stock	3,000,000	Estimated
Average	**2,895,833**	
Extrapolated enterprise total entropy (50 × average)	**144,791,650**	

The monthly enterprise information entropy is approximately 145 million bits.

Finally, consider the average retention of data across the business. A typical example would be 36 months. In which case, the total enterprise information entropy is simply the monthly estimate multiplied by the retention.

Enterprise information entropy (36 × monthly entropy):	**5,212,499,400**

Whether the average is adequately typical of all processes is a subject of useful professional debate. However, it provides the first baseline for this example enterprise of how much information is available each month to make business decisions: more than 5 billion bits of information! Another way of looking at this amount of information is to consider how many different states this represents or unique combinations of metrics it could correspond to. 5 billion bits is the same as roughly 2.5×10^{19}, or 25,000,000,000,000,000,000 different states!

This is a lot of information, but to understand how it is lost in the noise of the enterprise, consider that 5 billion bits of information require just 5 billion divided by eight bytes of storage, or just 625 megabytes. Since the average business measures storage in terabytes, even an organization with just ten terabytes of physical storage has a ratio of 625 megabytes on ten terabytes of useful and unique information—a ratio equivalent to just 0.00625 percent. No wonder the real information begins to look like the metaphoric needle in a haystack!

DECISION ENTROPY

While we can see that the enterprise information entropy is substantial, the amount of information used by decision makers is often very low. In fact, the amount is much lower than anyone might expect. That means there is a large amount of unused data in the organization. This becomes the latent opportunity of better management. There is a useful tension between a manager who drowns attempting to use all information and a manager who misses major decision-making opportunities by oversimplifying the business.

So how much information is a business executive using? The decision entropy is calculated on the values used by business managers that drive decisions—not the number of permutations that could be provided.

For example, Table 6.3 shows a typical sales report. The first four columns represent the information on three sales events for different items. Each row has a cost of manufacture, a sale price, and a derived absolute and percentage margin. In this simple example, business decisions are made on just the very last column, which represents a decision on whether the margin is within an arbitrary target range.

In this case, there are only two states (regardless of the amount of detailed information that was available) good or bad. The entropy of two states is $log_2 2 = 1$.

Table 6.3   Example Sales Report

				Analysis
Cost of Manufacture	Sale Price	Sale Margin	Margin Percentage	Good or Bad
$5,000	$10,000	$5,000	100%	Good
$7,000	$8,000	$1,000	14%	Bad
$6,000	$4,000	($2,000)	(33%)	Bad

Another typical example is of a business that records profit margin across a range of products to the nearest whole percentage point each month, with a range of −50 percent to +200 percent (i.e., 250 different potential values). In which case, the information entropy of each product profit report is $log_2 250$, or 7.97 bits. However, executives don't make a different decision based on whether the result is 23 percent or 24 percent. They would make a different decision if the result is −5 percent or +50 percent. Often, financial results are grouped in green, amber, or red (so-called traffic lighting). In this example, the business executive might say that less than 10 percent is red, 10 percent to 20 percent is amber, and greater than 20 percent is green. In which case, there are only three states that a product profit can hold, which equates to a decision entropy of $log_2 3$, or 1.58 bits. In this example, the decision entropy proportional to information entropy is defined to be:

$$\frac{Decision\ Entropy}{Information\ Entropy} = \frac{1.58}{7.97} = 0.20\ or\ 20\%$$

In other words, only 20 percent of the available detail is used to drive the decision. Could a more effective manager derive greater value by using more of the remaining 80 percent or would they drown in the detail?

These two examples imply, though, that that the decision entropy is of the same magnitude as the information entropy. However, that is seldom the case in the real world. Consider the case of the retailer we used as a working example in the previous section. The total enterprise information entropy was estimated to be 145 million bits per month. Let's consider what types of reports the managing director might be using of this business, again taking considerable creative license:

	Fields	Entropy	Instances	Entropy per Month
Monthly sales (by category)	10	200	50	10,000
Monthly turnover	5	100	10	1,000
Staff commission	5	150	500	75,000
Total				**86,000**

$$\frac{Decision\ Entropy}{Information\ Entropy} = \frac{86,000}{145,000,000} = 0.00059\ or\ 0.059\%$$

While the real business will have other reports and these numbers are simply guesses, they illustrate that only a tiny fraction of available information is being used. How little information is actually used for decision making is even more dramatic when compared to raw computer storage. Using the earlier example of ten terabytes, the example organization is making decisions using just 86,000 bits, or 0.00000011 percent of the total storage!

CONCLUSION AND APPLICATION

The information entropy analysis shows that while there is an overwhelming amount of raw computer storage, only a small fraction of that is actually available for decision making, and of that, only a small fraction again is actually used. In the example just given, a typical business (that might have had several terabytes of computer storage) had 5 billion bits of real usable information. That equates to only 625 megabytes of storage, or the equivalent of a small storage USB key! Even more dramatically, although the usable information is measured to be so small, only a fraction again is actually applied to the running of the business (in this example only 0.059 percent).

An analyst using the techniques of information entropy can identify opportunities for better business management or massive simplification of internal processes when data is being created with no executive application. Ultimately, information professionals can gain an understanding of best practice in the use of information in business decision making for each industry sector in which they work.

A thorough analysis of information in an organization needs to include all sources, including those that may have previously been overlooked because they are in an analog format, such as voice recordings and staff notes from client meetings.

Armed with this understanding, the information management strategy should focus on lifting both the enterprise information entropy and the decision entropy, and with them the total value of the information asset. Attempts to reengineer a business without focusing on the quantity of information and how it is used to make decisions are simply gambling on assumptions about the business.

NOTES

1. R. M. Losee (1997), "A Discipline Independent Definition of Information," *Journal of the American Society of Information Science*, 48(3): 254–269.
2. C. E. Shannon (July/October, 1948), "A Mathematical Theory of Communication," *Bell System Technical Journal*, 27: 379–423, 623–656.

Chapter 7

Describing the Enterprise

Data modeling often needs to be a labor of love, with many subtle twists and turns required to completely describe a business problem. Ted Codd defined the science and art of data modeling, starting with his paper "A Relational Model of Data for Large Shared Data Banks," as introduced in Chapter 4. The techniques continued to be developed through the 1970s and 1980s by many practitioners.

It used to be believed that it was possible to write a model for the entire organization—a so-called enterprise data model. Such a model would adhere to what's technically called third normal rules of normalization. Briefly, this means that the entities are related to each other in a unique way, avoiding the duplication of data and representing the business relationships in a completely generic way. Such an enterprise model is extremely attractive, providing flexible applications that consistently integrate. However, few businesses of any complexity have ever successfully developed such a model.

There are a number of reasons why the grand enterprise data model experiments have failed. First, to understand a data model it is necessary to understand all of the processes that use or populate the content. Such an analysis is a massive undertaking. Second, enterprise data models are an all-or-nothing affair; they do not prioritize. That is, even a minor entity can dramatically change the type of relationship. Finally, the data model is so much work that everyone assumes it is going to be a panacea for every information problem. The Small Worlds problem, also defined in Chapter 5, clearly shows that the data model is part of the problem, not the solution.

The following sections expand on these issues.

SIZE OF THE UNDERTAKING

Even a small business is akin to a complex machine with many moving parts. Although most organizations have a primary function, such as a retailer selling goods or a post office delivering letters, the closer you look, the more activities you see going on under the surface.

A business of a small retailer with just one shop might look straightforward with two primary processes: buy stock and sell stock. However, even a brief analysis will identify many other activities, such as hiring staff, rostering staff, paying staff, identifying suppliers, negotiating with suppliers, tracking shipments, processing customer credit, organizing accounts payable, and tax reporting. As anyone who has ever been involved in small retail knows, it is extremely competitive, so missing any information associated with any of these processes could incur extra expenses. For example, the retailer could pay too much for labor, stock, or credit and this could mean the difference between a profit and a loss.

For every process, there is a substantial amount of data. Even though much of the content is probably managed by packaged software, this data needs to be understood for the purposes of analysis.

Process	Example Associated Data
Hiring staff	Personal details, reference checks, skills
Rostering staff	Staff availability, historical customer traffic, skill levels
Paying staff	Pay, entitlements, loadings, leave accruals
Identifying suppliers	Third-party ratings, trade directories, competitor directors
Supplier negotiation	Supplier price history, contract breaches, competitor pricing
Shipment tracking	Stock dispatch details, shipping details
Customer credit	Personal details, past issues, gross profit
Accounts payable	Payment terms, past breaches, outstanding amounts
Tax reporting	Obligations, transaction details

ENTERPRISE DATA MODELS ARE ALL OR NOTHING

A very simple example to illustrate that data models cannot be built in isolation but must include all business processes is the relationship of product and price in a retailer. A modeler might initially argue that price is an attribute of the product but would soon notice the effect of inflation, which causes the price to increase over time (see Figure 7.1).

Once the shipment tracking process is analyzed, then it might be understood that products can be substituted for equivalents, creating a supply product and a sell product (see Figure 7.2).

Then the concept of member sales might be introduced, where customers with credit accounts are given preferential pricing during promotions. At that point, there are multiple prices that would further divide the price entity. Each additional analysis is likely to change fundamental relationships and entities.

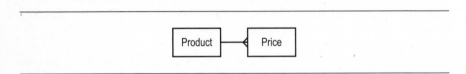

Figure 7.1 Product Price

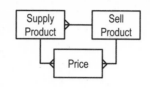

Figure 7.2   Product Price with Supply and Sell

Adding to the challenge, other processes are dependent on these entities. For instance, the tax analysis would link directly to both product and price, each change in these underlying entities would make the tax model redundant.

When Codd first proposed relational data modeling, he talked of shared data banks, since there were few databases that spanned multiple business applications at the time. While the concept of a relational model is very appealing from a theoretical standpoint, no evidence has been provided that it is universally able to be applied to large shared databases. While almost any problem can be described, it suffers from these challenges of exponential complexity.

THE DATA MODEL AS A PANACEA

Given the importance of data to the running of virtually any organization, it is no wonder that once an enterprise data modeling effort receives sponsorship, there are tremendous expectations on the capabilities the model will enable. Worse, as the effort continues to expand and the inevitable delays are announced, those expectations grow as well, only exceeded by the enthusiastic promises made by the data modeling team.

The complexity of enterprise data models are always underestimated, even by the most experienced data modelers. Inexperienced data modelers simply assume that the model will be a simple textbook representation of the business. More experienced data modelers have learned from the complexities they encountered in previous efforts, but they are still thrown by the exponential growth due to the subtle business process changes that exist in every organization.

Typically, the model that was anticipated to have 500 entities turns out to have more like 5,000. As a result, the Small Worlds metric issues that were introduced in Chapter 5 result in a model that is too big to be of any practical use to business executives, unless there is a substantial technical intervention. Meanwhile, so much funding has been used to create the model that there is no money left to allow technical staff to create systems that will actually use its complex structure.

METADATA

For any two individuals to talk, they must have some language in common. When a message is encoded for either real-time receipt or for future retrieval, there is much more context than the core message itself. For instance, a broadcast e-mail to your friends, "Come to a BBQ at our house on Saturday at 6," assumes your friend has additional context information. The abbreviation BBQ means barbeque and is short form for "have a meal with us that is going to be cooked (and probably eaten) outside using a barbeque." The word "our" in the invitation implies that your friend knows the sender is part of a family group and who the other members of the family group are. By putting "Saturday at 6," it is assumed that your friend will guess we mean this coming Saturday and we mean 6 P.M., not 6 A.M.

Consider the situation where a crowd is shouting at an individual, like the players on a sporting team all yelling at the umpire at the same time. The umpire is trying to hear above all the noise, looking for just a few key pieces of information. Like the barbeque invitation, there is a common language of the game, including key words specific to that sporting community (such as *goal*, *offside*, *try*, *point*, *hand ball*, and so on). There is a large amount of noise that the umpire needs to filter and only a few pieces of valuable information that he or she needs to absorb.

What's Said	What's Important
The #$*@ pushed me in the back!	Push in the back
He's offside now and was offside before!	Offside
The ball was over the line!	The ball is out
Are you blind, umpire?!?	—

Every enterprise has a common language of some sort that has evolved over a period of time, adopting both industry terms and phrases that have developed within the individual business. The senior executives of a business are in a similar situation as the sporting umpire, with a large number of people trying to provide information using the language of the enterprise to those executives.

Metadata, literally meaning data about data, is the language of the enterprise. Metadata should provide contextual information about every item or field of data held, although most metadata repositories are little more than dictionaries of field names providing a long-form description of the purpose of each item of information held. The metadata of the enterprise needs to assist in the aggregation and filtering of data to identify the most important elements in the sea of information.

Before we can determine what type of metadata is really needed, we need some way to quantify how much data there is and how much of it is actually used. While it is intellectually interesting to describe everything, if only a fraction of the enterprise content is useful, then the investment in effective metadata can be much more targeted.

While data should be objective (recording business events and observations), metadata can be tuned to the needs of the information consumer, making it subjective. For instance, a machinery manufacturer might record sale margin as the difference between cost of manufacture and the sale price:

Cost of Manufacture	Sale Price	Sale Margin
$5,000	$10,000	$5,000
$7,000	$8,000	$1,000
$6,000	$4,000	($2,000)

While the data records the simple fact of the margin amounts, the metadata can provide a level of interpretation. For instance, an executive might be interested in only the percentage margin and record anything less than 50 percent as a problem requiring further investigation.

			Interpretive Metadata	
Cost of Manufacture	Sale Price	Sale Margin	Interpretation: Margin Percentage	Interpretation: Good or Bad
$5,000	$10,000	$5,000	100%	Good
$7,000	$8,000	$1,000	14%	Bad
$6,000	$4,000	($2,000)	(33%)	Bad

The last two columns act as a lens on underlying data using metadata to derive a percentage and a rating. Using these columns, a manager can filter the raw sales information to drive a decision-making process. The percentage loses the underlying quantities and the interpretation is even less detailed, but both are much easier to work with than the raw numbers from which they were calculated.

Taken as a whole, the very large quantity of raw data available in an organization mimics complex systems found in nature, tempting us with powerful analogies to the worlds of physics and biology.

THE METADATA SOLUTION

As discussed in Chapter 6, not all content is of equal value or adds real information to the enterprise. While enterprise data models have to treat all data equally, metadata solutions don't have the same requirement. Metadata can focus on priority areas of the business. In addition, metadata models are not restricted to the same rules of normalization as data models, which means the Small Worlds problem is often able to be solved.

What is metadata? It is literally data about data. The tag *meta* (derived from the Greek word *after*) generally notes the concept *about* when used as an English prefix. While information management professionals agree on the name, that is about where agreement often ends. The biggest definition gap is between structured data practitioners who design relational data models and knowledge management experts who design repositories that span documents, e-mails, and other free-form content.

Particularly at issue is whether structured information about unstructured content should be defined as metadata. For example, the author (often a staff member) of a memo is metadata about the memo, the customer referred to in a loan application is metadata about the form, and the date an e-mail is sent is classified as metadata. The cause of this disparity of definition is the way that content is managed between the two groups. The structured data modelers created entities in their models to represent concepts of staff, customers, and even time to be associated with content around loans and communications, while the unstructured information managers record authorship, customer, and time in a structured list that indexes the original unstructured content.

An enterprise approach to metadata needs to span both and should take an inclusive rather than exclusive approach to metadata. Ultimately, the definition of metadata should not get lost in the semantics of different information management disciplines. Rather, it should be seen as potential information, as measured by information entropy, to be realized for decision making, as measured by the decision entropy.

MASTER DATA VERSUS METADATA

A particular aspect of inclusion that needs to be considered is the concept of master data. Master data management (MDM) has gained particular popularity due to the implementation of enterprise resource planning (ERP) systems in businesses. Such systems are designed to bring the financial management and business processes of an enterprise together in one integrated software solution. The common glue between divisions and modules of the software is the so-called master data, which describes aspects such as asset identifiers, customer numbers, staff numbers, locations, and other codes that are relatively static (compared to transactions and operational content). As described earlier, master data is generally in the realm of data rather than metadata by structured data modelers, but is definitely treated as metadata by managers of unstructured content.

In Chapter 8 we show that regardless of how master data is treated, it is definitely needed for free-form searches and so is a necessary part of the metadata search repository. It doesn't matter from an information management strategy perspective whether master data is classified as part of metadata, but it is essential that it is modeled as part of the same metadata solution.

MDM is discussed in more detail in Chapter 12.

THE METADATA MODEL

One thing that both the structured and unstructured information camps agree on is that metadata itself is structured and can be represented using a model. Further, it is generally agreed that the model is an association between objects not relational tables. This makes no practical difference, apart from the ability of objects to support many-to-many relationships, as shown in Figure 7.3.

The notation for the metadata object models should be the same as entity relationship models. For instance, a very simple Metadata model describing e-mail within an enterprise could look something like Figure 7.4.

In this example, one sender can generate multiple e-mails (referred to by a unique object identifier), while each e-mail could have multiple recipients. Of course, each recipient is likely to receive many individual e-mails; hence, there is a many-to-many relationship between e-mail and recipient, while an e-mail can only be sent by one sender (however, a sender can send multiple e-mails).

Returning to the school model described in Chapter 4, recall the data model to describe the relationship between parents, students, and teachers as described in Figure 7.5.

Using the techniques of Metadata modeling, we can now define a Metadata model for documents relating to a student and teacher, such as a report card, as shown in Figure 7.6. Using the data model of Figure 7.5, a parent wanting to identify the teachers they needed to see had to navigate six relationships, using the principles of verbs-and-nouns searches, which will be described in Chapter 8. The Metadata model will allow a direct association between all of the report cards for an individual student and the teachers who authored them with no room for the ambiguity of the original data model as shown in Figure 7.6.

A complete Metadata model for the same school needs to support the descriptions of the data model itself, which includes entities and attributes as well, as shown in Figure 7.7.

Such a model lends itself well to the creation of a metadata search repository with the inclusion of the concept of report, which is an aggregation

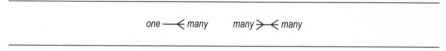

Figure 7.3   Relational versus Object Models

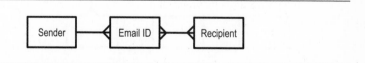

Figure 7.4   Simple E-mail Metadata Model

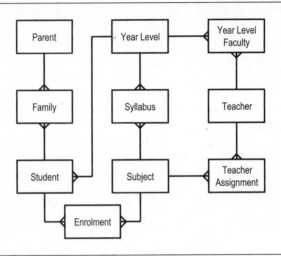

Figure 7.5   School ER Model

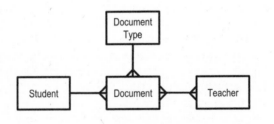

Figure 7.6   School Document Metadata Model

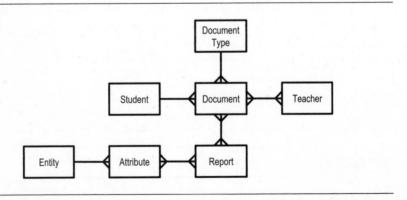

Figure 7.7   School Metadata Model

of attributes used to populate a query or report, such as a list of students and staff.

Another way to think about the use of metadata in this concept is as a shortcut between two distant entities within a data model. As with the parent/teacher example, modelers who are trying to integrate difficult concepts across a relational data model can use the Metadata model as a tool to aid navigation.

XML TAXONOMIES

XML (eXtensible Mark-up Language) provides another way of representing structured data, particularly when it is in motion between systems or people. XML is simply the representation of content in an ASCII file that includes the content, the name of the field, and the relationship between the fields. Each field is called a tag and the XML instance is called a document. For instance, a family might be represented as follows:

```
<family name="SMITH">
  <parents>
    <member dob="12 Dec 1965">John</member>
    <member dob="5 Jun 1968">Sally</member>
  </parents>
  <children>
    <member dob="1 Jun 1998">Chloe</member>
    <member dob="7 Sep 1999">Andrew</member>
  </children>
</family>
```

Use of XML allows for structured data to be moved around the organization with its metadata partially encoded and intact. This makes it very easy to manage content and to mine such documents using the same search tools that will be described in Chapter 8. Associated with XML documents should be schemas, which are, in effect, further metadata completing the description of the XML document structure. Ideally, any metadata model for the enterprise should acknowledge the existence of any schemas and recognize them as the master versions for the purpose of document validation.

METADATA STANDARDS

With so much debate about what should be included in metadata, it is little wonder that there are a few standards with varying degrees of acceptance. The good news, however, is that generally it is possible to work using existing standards as guide-lines and still build a Metadata model for the enterprise.

Some good examples of the type of standards that organizations need to consider include myriad XML standards, although eXtensible Business Reporting Language (XBRL)[1] is quickly becoming the most relevant for companies that do any kind of regulatory, financial, or market reporting.

XBRL should be adopted by every organization in those areas that collect, modify, or publish business financial or other performance-related data. The stan-dard makes Web pages containing financial results readable as structured data. This approach also allows businesses to exchange complex reporting information before the definition of every field has been agreed and defined.

Rather than publish a simple report, the underlying content is represented as XML, governed by a standard schema, and combined with extensions specific to the organization. The schema is shared with anyone wanting to understand the content in detail. For general readers, the content is transformed through Web tools into a standard-looking page. In fact, almost any document representation that is possible using these tools is also possible with XBRL content imbedded.

Another important standard is the Common Warehouse model (CWM),[2] which defines a standard metadata modeling approach for data warehousing tools that can be used to standardize access to the data warehouses and data marts.

Finally, the most important metadata standard available is arguably the well-accepted proposal developed by unstructured content practitioners: the Dublin Core Metadata Initiative.[3] Dublin Core has a foundation in ISO standard 15836 describ-ing 15 core data elements (the Dublin Core metadata element set). The 15 data elements are regarded as a minimum for describing any information resource or object (such as a document). They are: Contributor, Coverage (scope), Creator, Date, Description, Format, (unique) Identifier, Language, Publisher, Relation (related object), Rights, Source, Subject, Title, and Type (nature or genre).

The full description of the 15 data elements, and any future extensions, are main-tained as part of the Dublin Core Web site at http://dublincore.org/documents/dces.

Businesses will have made an enormous step toward the management of a sub-stantial proportion of their information if they can ensure that every document, e-mail, or Web page populates these 15 core elements. While they may appear daunting, most of them can have a default value that can be derived from the context in which the document was created or modified.

COLLABORATIVE METADATA

The trouble with data models is they need to be built in one single step, because any missing analysis can result in dramatic changes to the structure and potentially render invalid program code that is dependent on the database. In comparison, metadata is able to grow organically and is abstracted from the program code, which manages the content itself.

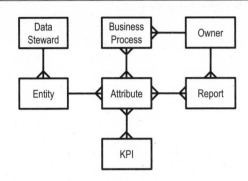

Figure 7.8 Initial Enterprise Metadata Model

One thing organizations can do, if they wish to invest in metadata, is to build collaborative metadata repositories, which allow staff to update the definitions and relationships themselves. Such a repository does not require particularly advanced technology and can be created using widely accepted and open collaboration tools, such as wikis.

A good starting point is a basic Metadata model, as shown in Figure 7.8.

This simple model will allow users of metadata to begin populating the metadata content using a wiki if a simple link is provided from each of the reporting and query tools that are available in the organization. A metadata administrator is needed to supervise the content as it is added, but it is advisable to make this a lag event rather than hold up publication based on the need for reviews.

The metadata repository will be even more powerful when hyperlinks to each element of content are available from within business applications, reports, and the intranet. Such an initiative quickly becomes self resourcing as more and more staff see the value it can bring to them in their day-to-day work.

The wiki as a collaborative authoring tool has been popularized by Wikipedia (www.wikipedia.org). Wiki technology is available free under open source licensing, or in commercial forms from various vendors. The concept is to provide Web pages that can be automatically populated (for instance, from an underlying metadata model) but also permit direct user edits.

Because all changes are tracked against users and are easily reversed, there is very little risk and a great deal of benefit for organizations embracing this model. In Chapter 8, a model is introduced to improve the usability of computer systems using search. This approach is particularly dependent on good metadata and there is a direct link between the way users maintain these pages and the experience they have using their business applications. Such a link provides a good motivation to regard metadata as a critical asset in its own right, as well as fundamental to the information asset in a more general way.

METADATA TECHNOLOGY

There are many metadata tools and repositories available on the commercial market with software also becoming available through open source initiatives. Due to the lack of standards, it is difficult for any technology department or CIO to mandate the use of just one solution. A more appropriate path is to define the underlying metadata model for the enterprise and monitor, encourage, and, where necessary, direct individual departments in their adoption of metadata technologies.

Some metadata resources, however, do need to be centralized. Of particular concern is the management of enterprise e-mail, given the responsibilities of organizations in different jurisdictions to comply with local laws covering discovery of electronic documents and messages.

As already described, the Dublin Core Metadata Initiative provides a rich foundation to build any metadata coding approach to enterprise documents like e-mail. An approach, however, that requires the user to manually fill in each of the 15 fields is unlikely to be successful. Worse, the abundance of storage and ease of attaching documents to e-mails makes it likely that the similar documents will multiply throughout the organization—each of which needs to be available to any court action. Ideally, this content would also be available to internal business development initiatives, although this is of a second order priority to compliance obligations.

The first step to gaining control is the establishment of unique identifiers on every type of document that are automatically generated the first time the document is saved. Incorporating this identifier in the metadata repository makes it very easy to implement some innovative techniques to reduce duplication and quickly populate the minimum metadata associated with every document.

The next step is to minimize duplication and attachment of files to e-mails. This is most simply done by using enterprise search tools and invoking them as a custom macro associated with the Attach button in the e-mail client and the save as option in the word processor. In both cases, search should provide a list of existing instances of the same document and invite the user to reference the existing instance rather than create a new one. While it should be easy to override, having such an option available to the user will often discourage unnecessary duplication.

The final measure to correctly identify each document is to use the same search as the document is created and then updated to understand the context, authorship, and relationships of the document. Because the Metadata model forms such a core part of the metadata search repository and already includes staff, document objects, divisions, and other relevant material, it is usually quite easy to automatically recommend default entries for each of the core metadata fields. The small investment in code for the enterprise will more than pay off in simplicity of document management in the future.

DATA QUALITY METADATA

Data quality is a governance issue in its own right. However, enterprise metadata provides the vehicle for recording objective metrics about the quality of different information resources. By making the metadata open and collaborative, different users of the same information can add their own commentary about its appropriateness for different uses and the assumptions they recommend in its application. For example, a customer database may be appropriate for selling additional services, but users may find that it is inadequately maintained to act as a reference for product recalls or other critical communications. Such measures also allow the business to prioritize ongoing investment in data quality by providing an integrated view of issues across the enterprise.

With good metadata in place, automated data quality measurement tools are also able to be applied, increasing the reliability of the content, which in turn will improve its usage and application beyond its original purpose.

HISTORY

Metadata is no different from any other form of dynamic information. The definition of items, their author, the granularity of relationships, and almost every other aspect of metadata has the potential to change over time. Some of these changes are relatively trivial and there is no real impact over time. For instance, changing the definition of sale price from "price that the goods were sold" to "price that the goods *or services* were sold" is unlikely to mean that the interpretation will materially change. Other changes, however, fundamentally change the way data needs to be analyzed. For instance, changing the definition of sale price from "price that the goods were sold" to "price that the goods were sold *including tax*" is very significant. Such a change might occur when a tax is implemented where one hasn't existed before.

While it could be argued that good modeling practice might be better served by keeping the definition of sale price consistent and adding a separate field, the reality is that it is often not possible, due to constraints of operational systems that weren't designed with the new tax in mind.

Figure 7.9 is an example of how such changes can be represented visually. The sales price data is still relatively comparable across years, but assuming that the new tax was applied in 2001, it is important to indicate that there was a change in definition at that point in time.

Each Metadata model needs to have the concept of time imbedded within it and a service that allows retrieval as a function of time. A simple way of programmatically showing changes in definitions, such as shown in Figure 7.9, is to add a surrogate key to the definition and to include it in the core data as a separate time series. In many analytical software packages, it is possible to include an

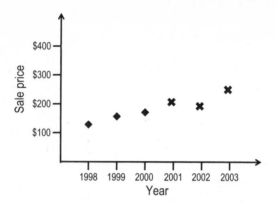

Figure 7.9   Showing the Change in Metadata

additional set of time series data and represent it by different icons or shapes, as seen in Figure 7.9.

Another concept that is often valuable to include in metadata is so-called exogenous events. An exogenous event is something that shapes the organization in some way and impacts definitions (such as changes to tax laws). Even changes to organization structure can be described in this way.

There is a valid argument to be had about whether exogenous events belong within metadata, master data, or within individual systems. From a general information management perspective, they should generally be available enterprise-wide, which makes them candidates for either metadata or master data. Because they often impact the way definitions are interpreted and results are framed, it often makes sense to describe them as metadata.

EXECUTIVE BUY-IN

The senior leadership of every organization should care a lot about the state of the metadata. Every day they are presented with complex analysis and reports from across the divisions of the business. Seldom do those spreadsheets, documents, or other resources make reference to their data source, the number of authors, or any evidence that the content wasn't completely fabricated.

Often a decision is made that will define the future of the company based on investment recommendations derived from complex spreadsheets. Increasingly, information-savvy executives want to know where the information came from and how it was derived so they can assign accountability to all of the contributors of the analysis. This makes middle managers more accountable and therefore more careful about the information they provide.

A proper approach to enterprise metadata allows the authors of reports and sponsors of investment recommendations to attribute the source of their data and codify the assumptions they have made. It also allows for the workings and assumptions to be checked by independent parties without reliance on the original authors—thus giving a greater degree of confidence to the result and the decisions that it drives.

The investment in metadata allows the leadership of any enterprise to prioritize and analyze investments in the information asset and ultimately in the organization itself. While many information management initiatives focus on consolidating and aggregating information that is already understood, it is often the metadata initiative that provides radical new insights by identifying data that has not been known to exist and linkages in the business that were previously hidden.

Ultimately, if executives believe in making fact-based decisions, they should insist that any material placed before them be properly and comprehensively referenced. Further, using those references, if a major decision is going to be made based on the content of the document, then a peer review can and should be undertaken. If the metadata is good enough, then the peer review can be blind—that is, the reviewer does not know who the original author is and vice versa.

NOTES

1. eXtensible Business Reporting Language governed by XBRL International. Available at www.xbrl.org.
2. Object Management Group (OMG), Common Warehouse Model (CWM). Available at www.omg.org/technology/cwm.
3. The Dublin Core Metadata Initiative (DCMI). Available at http://dublincore.org.

Chapter 8

A Model for Computing Based on Information Search

With metadata in place, there is much more that can be done beyond simply discovering the business meaning behind a data set that has already been identified. Metadata can drive the use of information and even dramatically improve the way computers are used to do almost every business task.

There is a phenomenal buzz around online search engine companies, which, to the casual observer, seems to be more related to hype around the Internet than any particularly strong business model. There must, however, be something that justifies the share price. Hype or not, these online search companies have the older technology businesses every bit as scared as they were in 1997 when they belatedly realized that the future was the Internet and not interconnected private networks, such as MSN and AOL. One thing is for sure, the smart money isn't betting on these businesses because of advertising revenue. While such income might be welcome, it isn't core business for the tech companies, who are scrambling to match the search engines function for function. To understand the motivation, it is worth rewinding to the early 1990s and the birth of the World Wide Web, as it is known today.

The first exposure that most early-adopting technology consumers had of the Internet was via a now long-gone technology called Gopher. Gopher was an Internet revolution, since, prior to its adoption, the only way to access resources had been to log directly onto the server (telnet). Gopher represented a set of server resources in a familiar tree structure, similar to the navigation we use for our own local hard disk drives.

Gopher can also be thought of in terms of the tree graphs introduced in Chapter 4, and is comparable to the first storage mechanisms for structured data. It isn't surprising that the approach to information navigation evolved in the same way as structured data to a full relational model.

Such an approach was invented by CERN (the European Organization for Nuclear Research) and quickly burst onto the scene: the World Wide Web. Developed by Tim Berners-Lee and Robert Cailliau, its development was motivated by a need to help researchers share information more effectively. Because the hypertext approach of the World Wide Web was so much better than anything that came before it, it was rapidly adopted as a standard. So much so that the terms *the Web* and *the Internet* are often used interchangeably.

Back in 1995, the way we used the Web was much more simplistic. Working on the basis that the Web is fully linked, users navigated (typically from their home page) one click at a time until they landed at their destination page. That probably sounds primitive, but it worked. So well that hundreds, if not thousands, of dot-com companies tried to leverage the paradigm in almost everything to create the information economy. The reason why this approach to clicking through sounds primitive is that today most of us start our Web experience at the search page. Even when we know our destination or task or URL, we still prefer a few choice keywords and to click from a list of options.

Now consider how most businesses work within the enterprise. The odds are that most people start their day looking at a list of application icons, clicking through an Intranet to a hard-to-find application link, or searching through dozens of favorites they've filed under some obscure name. Much of their time is probably spent looking for that one function they only perform every few months. Unlike the Internet, workplaces are application-centric rather than oriented around information. This is despite all of the hype around empowering knowledgeable workers and putting control of business computing in the hands of the end-user.

FUNCTION-CENTRIC APPLICATIONS

In general, people don't question the status quo. Workplaces are like this because it is how everyone does it. Just because it is the norm does not make it the right way to do business, particularly when you consider that the vast majority of any organization's infrastructure is dedicated to storing data that can be used in a multitude of ways, that is, databases like data warehouses, spreadsheets, and analysis documents. Just like the Internet, most organizations keep a vast amount of information in various states of aggregation. Unlike the Internet, it isn't assumed that a worker's first thought is for the data—rather, it is assumed they will navigate to an application that manages the data that is of interest.

In the 1970s and 1980s, there was little data involved in computer applications. Users loaded or accessed an application, such as general ledger, stock control, or payroll. With the application open, they were then presented with a set of functions, often numbered as in Figure 8.1.

Designers of modern computing interfaces, including the Intranet, have focused on making the application functions easier to navigate and have often provided innovative user interfaces based on the concept of portals, which dynamically change the information on the screen based on usage history of the individual user. Such user interfaces are a far cry from the question-and-answer-style forms with numbered options, which were available to earlier generations of business users.

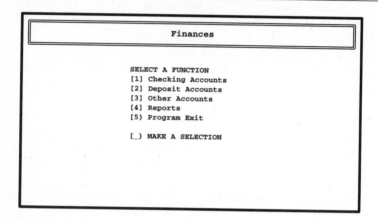

Figure 8.1   Typical 1980s Application

Such interfaces, however, are only useful if users know how to find them. While that is easy for major applications an individual might use every day, it is a much bigger problem when the task is done infrequently. For instance, it can be expected that the accounts payable clerk will know exactly where to find the application for generating a vendor payment. The same clerk, however, probably doesn't know with the same confidence how to look up their annual leave balance.

AN INFORMATION-CENTRIC BUSINESS

A new class of enterprise search tools is beginning to change the end-users' working experience every bit as dramatically as the move from mainframe menus to desktop applications and again to Web-based applications. Instead of starting their day with a series of application icons, the user is starting from a clean search screen. Using a combination of natural language terms, including verbs (such as *register, order,* and *find*), nouns (such as *purchase order, invoice,* and *customer*), and proper nouns (such as *John Smith* and *Acmi Co.*), they undertake tasks. Search results are not ranked by programmer but by usage with some bias by application owners. Searching includes not only the content of documents but also the attributes of databases and the content itself. Results include the applications that are used to perform a function, queries that have been written that can be used to find data and documents, or spreadsheets that have been used to analyze information.

The organization that can structure its business around information is better equipped to compete in an information economy. Most workers have little idea how to find information outside of their core job function, and few managers are aware of what analysis has been done by others. The most common response to a new request for information is to build a new data collection spreadsheet accompanied by a set of assumptions and sample extrapolation. The new spreadsheet is often a partial or complete duplicate of another middle manager's previous efforts!

Information research skills are not generally taught as part of core training programs. In fact, most people think in terms of information before they think about business process. Consider the following situations:

The customer of a utility company rings the call center with a query about their bill. The customer service operator who takes their call should have access to information about all of their past bills and details of any prior interactions with the company. In looking at this information, the operator should be able to prioritize based on key phrases that the customer gives them, such as "over charging" (which might highlight earlier such complaints). Instead of being provided with such a free-form system, call center staff are almost always directed to use a point-and-click set of selections that requires them to identify the pre-programmed query the customer requires. Even if the customer's question is a close match to the canned options, there is usually a substantial number of clicks and associated delay. Worse, if the customer's question takes the operator away from the standard questions, a supervisor needs to get involved, and often data collection is beyond the resources available to the call center team.

A business client of a bank declares bankruptcy and the loan officers have a mad scramble to work out what the bank's exposure is to the client. Anyone who has worked in banking will know that all but the smallest institutions have many systems and reporting databases covering a vast array of complex financial products. The bank could be exposed to an individual client (including their subsidiaries) in any one of these. The staff member trying to bring the picture together quickly needs to know how to access those systems (many of which they don't use day-to-day) and draw on a list of reports and spreadsheets to deduce the total position.

Data warehouse practitioners would point out that, at the present time, the correct solution is to implement an enterprise data warehouse to consolidate all of the information in a consistent, integrated, and structured form. While this investment is well worthwhile, the reality is that such a solution is incomplete for almost all real businesses and can only form part of the answer. Further, a data warehouse is about information in the reporting sense only and doesn't provide access to the underlying applications.

ENTERPRISE SEARCH

Humans think well in natural language. Ask someone to do a task on the Internet, such as check the weather for today, and they are likely to start at a search screen (like www.google.com) and type "Melbourne weather for today," with the correct result (in the case of the author's home town, www.bom.gov.au) coming up in the first few returned links. In this case, the first two words of the search, "Melbourne" and "weather," are metadata items. They describe the data set we are looking for. The additional words "for" and "today" provide context, which clever modeling will help provide the user with more accurate results.

Enterprise search is neither magic nor a panacea. Any researcher who makes regular use of the Internet will know they have to use multiple search engines, and even then are likely to be missing key pieces of information. However, with the pace of information growth within the enterprise outpacing any attempt to manually fit it into a structure, anything that provides an automatic and heuristic indexing mechanism is a great start.

The information managers in an organization cannot, however, simply implement a search engine and let their users loose without some degree of planning and design.

SECURITY

Information should be as widely available as possible; however, better access to information introduces new security issues. One of the most common surprises for businesses that are implementing such solutions is the sudden appearance of sensitive information in open searches. While a search engine shouldn't make information visible that is in secure locations, it is surprising how much confidential data is loaded into spreadsheets and other documents and left on unsecured and shared computer network drives on the basis that the directory structure is sufficiently complex that no one is likely to ever find it. This is equivalent to leaving a key to your house outside under a stone, its security based on the number of stones in the garden. Imagine if you had some type of key detection system at the front gate that allowed anyone to search your garden automatically—suddenly your hidden key strategy doesn't seem so sensible!

Information managers should take the time to implement good security practices and educate staff on the need to protect enterprise information assets. More complex security issues also arise, such as whether to allow the indexing of information that is within secured sections of the computer network. While it is tempting to give a search engine free reign over all content on the enterprise networks, a more conservative and targeted strategy is to build a metadata repository and start by indexing just the content of the repository and the associated open access documents. A discussion on security covers these topics more thoroughly in Chapter 14.

METADATA SEARCH REPOSITORY

The metadata search repository is a subset of enterprise metadata and is just focused on providing material that can be consistently indexed and cross-referenced to key business resources. Such resources include documents, Intranet pages, spreadsheets, business applications, and reporting databases.

Documents	Businesses generate vast quantities of documents, usually drafted in word processors and in various states of draft through to final.
Intranet pages	While the World Wide Web has become increasingly interactive and easily searchable, intranets still rely on staff knowing where to find the pages they're after.
Spreadsheets	Tens of thousands, if not hundreds of thousands, of spreadsheets are created every year by company workers to tackle everything from data analysis to annual reporting. Many of these spreadsheets become data sources in their own right.
Business applications	Similar business functions are often implemented using different computer applications within the same organization. Staff often know how to find only one or two of these applications.
Reporting databases	Apart from spreadsheets, many small and large databases are created, including data warehouses and datamarts. These repositories of structured data contain information about customers, staff, financial results, and virtually everything else that the business does. Despite the substantial investment organizations make in this technology, usually only a fraction of their potential users even knows where to find the right reporting tools.

A metadata search repository brings these concepts together into a searchable index that is then able to be used as a launching point for the source documents or systems. Technically, such a repository need be nothing more than a set of ASCII[1] or text-based files that contain the key metadata items. The objective is to make it easy for a search engine indexing the metadata search repository to support natural language phrases.

When designing a metadata search repository for an individual organization, consider what information is in the user's mind when they are likely to want to do certain things. Some examples might include customer details, department or division, product details, and metrics (such as profit, sales, or customer numbers). A standard file can then be created that will include all the keywords extracted from these categories with one file created for each object that is being indexed. For instance, a telecommunications company might have a standard financial report that includes details for home phone products covering the consumer market (customer categories A, B, and C), so the file might look something like this:

Object: Sales report fulfillment
Customer category A, customer category B, customer category C
All care phone, home phone standard, home phone premium
Link: http://financialreports.intranet.xyz.com/sales_reports

A database of phone repairs would list not just the application but also every customer against whom it could be applied. The inclusion of every possible customer might seem excessive for an ASCII file, but it is important to remember that even if the organization has 10 million relevant customers, the resulting ASCII file is likely to be no bigger than 10 million (number of customers) times 15 bytes (average name length), or 150 million characters, equating to just 150 megabytes, which is not large by computing standards.

Object: Customer repairs (business application)
Customer category B, customer category C
All care phone, home phone premium
Link: http://customerepairs.intranet.xyz.com
John Alfred, Anne Andrews, Martin Aston ... Mark Zornes....

BUILDING THE EXTRACTS

It is also important to remember that these files do not need to be maintained in real-time and can be extracted and maintained by simple batch processes on an irregular basis. The intention should be that they are inclusive rather than exclusive. In other words, they will err toward finding objects that are not relevant rather than worry about whether every object is relevant for every customer. The files are simply an amalgam of the metadata, or customer items, that are possibly relevant. For each major category of application or report, the potential customers should be extracted from some kind of master source (such as the customer table). If the number of files is becoming excessive, then more than one link can be provided in the same file. When in doubt, keywords should include everything that could possibly be relevant.

The extracts themselves are largely a matter of building SQL to extract details from structured repositories and grouping together collections of spreadsheets (encouraging new authors to post to the correct locations). Over time, documents and spreadsheets can be indexed directly. Ideally, a heuristic correction process should also be introduced allowing users to tailor the keywords and customer categories in an individual file to better target the object that it represents.

THE RESULT

While the initial file extract approach to the search repository is a stop-gap measure, over time it should be embedded in the enterprise metadata repository (see Chapter 7). Even this short-term measure, however, will achieve the goal of creating a useful natural language interface that will allow staff to find the application, report, or spreadsheet that is directly relevant to their task. For instance:

Search	Finds
Home loan for John Smith	• Reports that can be run against a data warehouse or reporting database summarizing John Smith's loan • Original loan documents • Business system that allows for maintenance of John Smith's customer details
Phone number for Adam Brown	If Adam is a staff member and a customer it will find: • Business system containing customer contact details and relationship managers • HR systems containing HR contact points • Internal phone directory
Loss given default of XYZ Corporation	• A report (or reports) from the data warehouse showing the risks associated with XYZ Corporation (including subsidiaries) • A list of business systems used to enter and maintain facility and collateral information for XYZ Corporation

Such a search solution soon overtakes the Intranet's home page as the starting point of choice for staff and encourages a culture change from thinking first about the application to considering the information that is relevant to the business problem at hand.

Often, such an approach also has the benefit of teaching people how to do a task better or allowing them to find information they would not even know they needed. As with the Internet, search engines return an ordered list of relevant items. While the main link users are looking for is usually near the top, over time, staff start to look more closely at some of the other items that are proposed by the search engine and even start to ask questions about whether things are as they should be. That way, every staff member becomes an information manager in their own right.

Much of the approach described in this chapter is enabled by a concept called Web 2.0. The label appears to have been first used by Tim O'Reilly in about 2004, and he defined it in 2006 as follows:

Web 2.0 is the business revolution in the computer industry caused by the move to the Internet as platform, and an attempt to understand the rules for success on that new platform.

This definition builds on the idea of the Internet as an interactive medium that has strong semantic metadata. As a result, pages contain far more than information for consumption and include the algorithms that define the content, making them active and searchable.

With interactive metadata, the content is able to evolve and be maintained by the user community rather than relying solely on an administrator or team of programmers. Such a model for computing is far more sustainable and creates a more relevant set of business solutions. In Chapter 3, the concept of information governance was introduced and included the content lifecycle, which such an approach to dynamic systems helps to manage very effectively.

NOTE

1. American Standard Code for Information Interchange (ASCII) is a character encoding standard based on the English alphabet and excluding any formatting.

Chapter 9

Complexity, Chaos, and System Dynamics

In the late nineteenth century, mankind was enormously confident in its mastery of the physical world. Engineers were reshaping society and physicists were confident they were masters of their universe. Only a few small niggles remained. For instance, no matter how carefully the orbit of Mercury was plotted, it never quite matched the equations, and there was also the strange behavior of light, which seemed to act like both a wave and a particle—but everyone was confident consistent explanations were close. Newtonian physics was king and no challenge was even contemplated.

Then, at the dawn of the twentieth century, an upstart patents clerk knocked over the first domino with the special theory of relativity, and the rest is history. (By the way, Einstein's slightly later general theory of relativity explains the minor inconsistency in the orbit of Mercury through the curvature of space-time.) We now know that Newtonian physics gives a very good description of the world that we deal in every day at the scale of millimeters through to kilometers but that it breaks down when we deal with the very small in particular (and, to a lesser extent, the very large).

Einstein's major contribution was the concept that the one constant of the universe is the speed of light and all else is measured relative to that. In fact, although it is usually described in terms of the speed of light, the foundation of the relativity is in fact a limit on the speed with which information can be shared between points. The speed of light is also the maximum speed of information transmission.

EARLY INFORMATION MANAGEMENT

Early forms of information management revolved around the Dewey Decimal System, which is, in itself, a form of tree graph with each digit fine-tuning the one to the left, as described in Chapter 4.

When John F. Kennedy launched the mission to put a man on the moon, he did much more than that. He also created one of the largest logistical projects of the century. NASA had to find ways to manage the millions of independent components being manufactured by hundreds of different contractors for the rocket and spacecraft required by the mission. By the time Neil Armstrong set foot on the moon in 1969, IBM had also introduced the first major hierarchical data storage system, called IMS (for Information Management System), developed in order to handle the huge bill of materials associated with the Saturn V rocket.

IMS was not the first database product (called then a data bank or data base in two words), but it did encapsulate all of the principles of the data bank of the era.

First, it was focused on supporting hierarchical concepts (e.g., an engine is made up of multiple parts that, in turn, have multiple components). Such a structure is consistent with the early information management principles espoused in systems, such as the Dewey Decimal approach to categorizing data. Second, it was designed to support specific business processes. The developers of IMS were improving on program-specific data storage techniques that largely existed until that time. The concept of data in its own right did not exist. Hierarchical systems of storing data have only two directions that any change can be applied, down or up the tree graph. As such, it is straightforward to predict the impact of any action or change.

SIMPLE SPREADSHEETS

Anecdotally, the majority of information management initiatives seem to start life as haphazard spreadsheets that are applied to one or two small departments or groups within the enterprise. Sometimes this is by evolution, where a good idea is born at the departmental level and put together by an enthusiastic graduate. Other times, it is by design, where there is a deliberate plan to prototype the theory or initiative within a controlled environment. All too often, the resulting spreadsheet, which purports to solve a marketing, risk, product, or other problem, is presented to the information technology team, and they are instructed simply to scale it up to the enterprise. They usually seem to fail. The failure of the technologists to achieve the objectives of the small prototype at the enterprise scale is used as evidence by the business of the incompetence of the technology department. While they may sometimes be right, there are fundamental reasons why they are doomed to fail in this type of endeavor.

The nineteenth-century physicists were right when they claimed they could use Newtonian principles to predict almost every action of bodies in motion or at rest at the scales they were familiar. When, however, the scale of object is dropped by several orders of magnitude, strange things start to happen and we enter the realm of quantum mechanics. In this space, statistics rather than deterministic mathematics decide the location and momentum of objects.

Similarly, we are finding that information management follows the same principles. At the small scales of a few lists with thousands or even tens of thousands of records, it is relatively easy to predict what will happen. At much larger scales, things start to get much harder.

COMPLEXITY

Warren Weaver, a contemporary of Claude Shannon, was an early advocate of understanding complex systems and believed they would apply across science, including the use of computers. Writing in *American Scientist* in 1948[1] Weaver described science before 1900 as "largely concerned with two-variable problems of simplicity," and went on to introduce, for the first time, a new term, *organized complexity*. He saw the advent of the computer, combined with skills developed during the Second World War, as allowing humanity, for the first time, to tackle very complex problems combining multiple nonlinear components, and for which the mathematical outcome was anything but obvious.

Typical of his time, most scientists believed that complex systems tended to organize themselves in such a way as to achieve a macroscopic outcome that was predictable once the statistics of the constituent parts was understood. Hence, when complexity is discussed, it is often in terms of Weaver's organized complexity, identifying such a structured outcome from a massive quantity of variables with complex nonlinear interactions.

Scientists were particularly interested, in the lead-up to the discovery of DNA, in the systematic way in which complex organisms seemed to operate, despite being made up of massive numbers of independent components. It was largely this experience that gave the mid-twentieth-century scientist confidence that increasing the number of variables made the outcome more subtle but still ultimately predictable.

CHAOS THEORY

Chaos theory is used to understand and make predictions about the apparently random behavior of complex systems with interacting nonlinear components. The key aspect of chaotic systems is that they are very sensitive to even small changes of initial conditions. This means that nearly identical systems, with only slight differences, will quickly behave very differently. The principles of contemporary Chaos theory began to be developed in the 1960s when weather forecasters were attempting to produce a series of mathematical tools that would comprehensively predict the weather, not only for days, but months or even years ahead.

This effort led to the finding that models that accurately mimicked the real world could be developed. However, any variation in the input conditions, even at the finest level of accuracy, caused wild variations in the predicted weather outcome in just days or even hours. The mathematician Edward Lorenz coined the term *the butterfly effect*, as it is often explained using the notion that a butterfly stirring the air today in Beijing might transform storm systems next month in New York. Lorenz stumbled upon chaos while investigating models used for meteorological prediction, later saying:

The average person, seeing that we can predict tides pretty well a few months ahead would say, why can't we do the same thing with the atmosphere, it's just a different fluid system, the laws are about as complicated. But I realized that any physical system that behaved non-periodically would be unpredictable.[2]

Researchers have gone on to build much simpler systems and discovered the same effect, ultimately coming to the conclusion that any system with many non-linear interacting components is a candidate for chaos. Chaos theory has been applied to the analysis of many different types of systems. To date, the most common application is to biological and mechanical systems. The value of Chaos theory is that apparent random behavior of a chaotic system can usually be explained by a set of deterministic nonlinear rules. In some circumstances, this can mean the unpredictable behavior of a system can be avoided by careful manipulation of certain parameters.

Complexity theory can then be broken into two subject areas—organized complexity, covering those Weaver systems that have many nonlinear components but fall into a stable pattern of behavior, and chaotic systems that have apparently similar structures but, despite coherent results, do not ever fall into a stable pattern.

WHY INFORMATION IS COMPLEX

The principles of shared data, fundamental to the concept of relational data models, introduce a whole new paradigm. Rather than having two directions (up or down), relational data models support an unlimited number of relationships. The types of relationships are also more complex with one-to-many cardinality being supported in any direction. Such a structure implies nonlinear relationships between each of the entities—the precursor to showing the existence of complex and potentially chaotic behavior.

Where a hierarchical approach to storing data is akin to managing a bill of materials (such as the components of a Saturn V rocket), the relational database is designed to concurrently share the dynamic and real-time content of many different transactions across different lines of business.

It is difficult to prove for all data models that they are potentially complex or chaotic, but it is possible to provide an indication for specific cases. Consider two entities, A and B, drawn in Figure 9.1 as entities and then in Figure 9.2 as a graph.

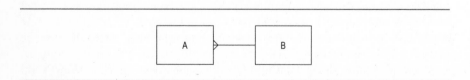

Figure 9.1   Simple Entity Relationship Diagram

Figure 9.2 Simple Entity Relationship as a Graph

Figure 9.3 Relationship with an Intermediary

Denote A_n and B_n to refer to the number of elements in the entities respectively. The number of possible values for the relationships between the two entities is therefore:

$$A_n B_n$$

This overlap can be thought of as the glue, or attraction, that binds sets A and B together. For a given population, there is unlikely to be an even distribution of relationships. For instance, if entity A represents students and B teachers, then some teachers have more students in their classes. In which case, the number of distinct values is a defined proportion of $A_n B_n$. Call the proportion P and the new measure of attraction is:

$$PA_n B_n$$

Of course, there is a relationship between entities even when there is an intermediary entity, arbitrarily called C for the purpose of this calculation (see Figure 9.3).

Intermediary entities, at best, maintain all of the relationships between the entities they separate but can be assumed to filter a proportion according to an undefined function (determined by the individual situation), arbitrarily called $F()$, where $F()$ is a function to be determined.

At a distance of 1, the function should be inserted exactly zero times (as there is no intermediation), represented by $F^0()$. At a distance of 2, there is one intermediation represented by $F^1()$, and so on, generically written as $F^{d-1}()$, where d is the geodesic distance between A and B. As a reminder, geodesic distance means the smallest number of edges or joins (in the case of Figure 9.3, this is 2).

In a specific example, $F()$ could be a simple linear function of d itself, which would mean at a geodesic distance of 3 it could be represented as Kd^2, where K is an arbitrary function. In this case, the strength of the relationship could be described as:

$$\frac{PA_nB_n}{Kd^2}$$

Students of physics would recognize the similarity of this structure with the gravitational attraction equation:

$$F = \frac{GMm}{r^2}$$

If A is under the influence of another entity with roughly the same properties, then there is now the simple equivalent of the three-body gravitational problem. This is a problem in mathematics and physics; while apparently simple to describe the three-body gravitational situation has proven impossible to date to solve with a discrete set of equations, implying that the solution does not settle into a defined or predictable set of relationships.

Even if the data itself is not shown to have complex and potentially chaotic relationships, the processes that populate it can rapidly develop such a behavior. Even when information might be stable, it is important to remember that it is the result of a process. Recall Robert Losee's definition of information described in Chapter 6:

> Information is produced by all processes and it is the values of characteristics in the processes' output that are information.

To demonstrate how quickly a system can become both complex and chaotic consider a data warehouse that is loaded through a batch process. The following is drawn from a paper titled "The Implications of Chaos Theory on the Management of a Data Warehouse,"[3] written by the author and co-authored by Peter Blecher and Peter O'Donnell of Monash University.

In order to demonstrate that data warehouses are subject to chaotic behavior, a very simple model can be constructed using just two major interacting variables to represent the number of active queries and the amount of data loaded. The model describes a data warehouse with just one source of data and attempts to describe the length of time taken to complete the daily load and the number of queries processed each day.

The following assumptions define the behavior of the data warehouse described by the model: the more queries running while the load is running, the longer the load will take; the more data loaded, the more queries will be submitted; the later the load finishes, the more queries will be submitted the next day (to fulfill unmet demand); and if more queries run on one day, less queries will be run the next day. These assumptions should be realized in the model by the two primary equations to describe the number of active queries (Q) and volume of data loaded (L) loaded at any given time (t).

$$Q_t = aT_f + bL_{t-1} - dQ_f$$

$$L_t = L_{t-1} + c\left(1 - \frac{Q_t}{aT_{day} + bL_{max} - dQ_f}\right)$$

Table 9.1 describes each of the coefficients and parameters.

Using these equations and coefficients, the model is simple to construct in any one of the commonly available development environments, including Microsoft Access (as undertaken for the original paper) or using system dynamics, as described later in this chapter.

To indicate how sensitive the model is, and by extension real-world data environments, Table 9.2 shows two sets of parameters. The first is stable while the second displays chaotic and unacceptable behavior from a user perspective. The model was run with T_{day} set to 1,440 (equivalent to the number of minutes in a day).

While this model is a substantial simplification on real-world data warehouses, it shows most of the important behaviors exhibited by such systems. Depending on the values assigned to each of the coefficients, the key measures (time of completion and total queries processed in a day) either stabilize after a period of time or remain unstable. In the latter case, the key measures often do not repeat, regardless of the

Table 9.1   Coefficients and Parameters

a	Relates the extra queries submitted in this day due to the lateness of finishing the previous day
b	Relates the relationship between the amount of data loaded today and the number of queries submitted (the more data that is loaded, the more queries will be submitted)
c	Represents the volume of data that would be loaded in each time interval if there were no queries running
d	Relates the reduction in queries submitted today due to the number that were executed the previous day
T_f	The time the load finished the previous day (zero for the first day). T_f is non-integer, which means that the partial unit is calculated as $(t-1) + \dfrac{(L_{t-L_{t-1}})}{(L_{max} - L_{t-1})}$
Q_f	The total queries executed the previous day (zero for the first day)
T_{day}	The number of time intervals (t) in a day
L_{max}	Volume of data required to be loaded before the process is complete for the day

Table 9.2   Different Sets of Model Parameters

Parameter	Set A—stable	Set B—unstable
a	0.009	0.009
b	0.0005	0.0005
c	15	14
d	0.0005	0.0005
Normal query rate	0.1	0.18
Load target	5000	5500

length of the experiment, hence the system exhibits chaotic rather than periodic behavior. Interestingly, regardless of whether the system eventually stabilizes, there are often performance spikes that appear to have little impact on subsequent days. The physical equivalence of this phenomenon may be the bad days that data warehouse managers sometimes experience, where their system inexplicably performs badly and then quickly returns to normal.

Given that this simplified data warehouse model can be easily configured to exhibit chaotic behavior, it is reasonable to extrapolate the finding to real-world data warehouses that contain the same basic principles but have additional influences making them even more complex.

EXTENDING A PROTOTYPE

Consider a national chain of clothing stores that decides to trial a loyalty card. To prove the concept, the marketing team develops a spreadsheet system to manage the customers for one store. The first version is a simple list, an example of which is shown in Table 9.3.

Such a scheme is often a great success, so the prototype is extended to another store. Both stores maintain their own spreadsheet, and in the event of the occasional conflict where the same customer registers in both stores, a single phone call is all that is needed to consolidate the record into one or other list. Such a system is hierarchical in that there are no links between the parent entity stores.

Even the next logical extension, recording the individual sales and redemptions made to a given customer, is linear and hierarchical, as shown in Figure 9.4.

To illustrate the linear nature of the relationships, the number of sales transactions and point redemptions is a multiple of the number of customers by the average number of sales or redemptions per customer. Similarly, the number of customers is a simple multiple of the number of stores by the average number of customers per store.

Now consider the task of generalizing the spreadsheets to the entire organization. The designers face two options: either maintain the business model with its obvious issues of customer duplication or convert the model from a hierarchical structure to a relational model. The first option involves a dramatic growth in the number of instances of the customer and (assuming the rollout increases the

Table 9.3 Simple Points Prototype

Name	Address	Points
Anne Barry	1 Chester Street, Doncaster	539
Ellen Foster	87 Graham Street, Hotham	9,097
Irene Jacobs	50 Kitchener Road, Longreach	5,300
...	...	...

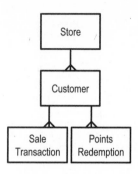

Figure 9.4 Prototype Data Model

program's publicity) a growth in the number of customers per store. Assume, for the sake of argument, that the chain has 100 stores nationally and that each store maintains a list of 10,000 names (a reasonable estimate for a viable business). Assume further that 10 percent of customers visit a second store twice a year and seek to add their transaction to their home store or use points from their home store. Either event requires a manual matching of their customer details (which equates to 200,000 manual phone calls across the country each year). Also assume that, due to congestion, other duties, and human error, 5 percent of all manual matches across the country are incorrectly completed (this is a conservative estimate and roughly aligns to the best research on the average spreadsheet error rate).[4] Conservatively, such an approach would result in 10,000 errors each year with a skew toward the business's best customers (who are the most likely to interact with the company). Most designers would decide that such an approach has an unacceptable error rate and would abandon the hierarchical approach in favor of a relational approach.

Now the model looks more like a customer interacting with multiple stores as shown in Figure 9.5.

Any enterprise-level solution with customer information that can be updated from multiple sites needs to audit those updates, since they are beyond the control of an individual store and may need to be reconciled if there is a dispute. As shown in the ER diagram, each store can perform multiple customer updates, and similarly, each customer can have multiple updates. A sale transaction needs to be associated with both a customer and a store, as do point redemptions.

Now, however, the relationship of customers to stores is a complex function of three resolving entities (customer update, sale transaction, and points redemption). Any attempt to estimate the number of customers based on store numbers using this model relies on functions of customer update, sale transaction, and points redemption. Because each of these three resolving entities crosses both store and customer boundaries, the relationship function is necessarily nonlinear—that is, the

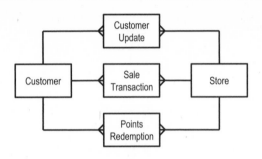

Figure 9.5   Scaled-up Data Model

relationship is not a simple count of averages, as it was in the prototype model in Figure 9.4.

The existence of multiple nonlinear interactions between the entities is not sufficient to demonstrate chaotic behavior, but it is an indicator of the possibility of such a situation. To illustrate how much more complex the production model in Figure 9.5 is, consider the testing required in each case. The principle of test case management is that each state a system can exist in is considered and tested. For the data, this means describing each combination of one or more records. In Table 9.4, the different meaningful combinations are described. Each cell has the value 0, 1, or M, representing no records, one record, or many records, respectively. For the prototype model, test cases only require a maximum of one record in order to test permissible values, since a customer can belong to only one store and sale transactions are allocated only to customers. In the production model, however, that constraint has been moved and a nonlinear relationship has been created associating customers and stores via three intermediary entities (customer update, sale transaction, and points redemption). In this case, the situation has to be tested where at least one or other of store or customer is related in the multiple.

Any actual existence of chaotic behavior will depend on the business rules that populate the entities, but the opportunity is created by these complex relationships for such a result. Just as significantly, the five test cases required to properly test the prototype system grow to 34 in the case of the production model.

SYSTEM DYNAMICS

The data model simply records the state of data at a point in time and reflects the content created by business processes and activities. Because, however, the purpose of relational models is to constrain or enable business rules through the relationships, the capability for nonlinear interactions is a factor of the data model.

Table 9.4 Test Cases

Prototype Model				Production Model				
Store	Customer	Sale Transaction	Points Redemption	Store	Customer	Customer Update	Sale Transaction	Points Redemption
0	0	0	0	0	0	0	0	0
1	0	0	0	1	0	0	0	0
1	1	0	0	0	1	0	0	0
1	1	1	0	1	1	1	0	0
1	1	1	1	1	1	0	1	0
				1	1	0	0	1
				1	1	1	1	0
				1	1	0	1	1
				1	1	1	0	1
				1	1	1	1	1
				M	1	M	0	0
				M	1	0	M	0
				M	1	0	0	M
				M	1	M	1	0
				M	1	1	M	0
				M	1	0	M	1
				M	1	0	1	M
				M	1	M	0	1
				M	1	1	0	M
				M	1	M	1	1
				M	1	1	M	1
				M	1	1	1	M
				1	M	M	0	0
				1	M	0	M	0
				1	1	0	0	M
				1	M	M	1	0
				1	M	1	M	0
				1	M	0	M	1
				1	M	0	1	M
				1	M	M	0	1
				1	M	1	0	M
				1	M	M	1	1
				1	M	1	M	1
				1	M	1	1	M

One technique to understand the content and structure of a data model is to use a system dynamics simulation. System dynamics is a form of simulation that allows stocks and flows to be interconnected, including the creation of feedback loops. The technique was invented by Jay Forrester in the late 1950s, and while a very simple concept, a short time spent working with the technique shows its power. Figure 9.6 shows an easy way to visualize system dynamics, with stocks being represented by containers of fluid and flows being variable taps that permit fluid flow between the containers.

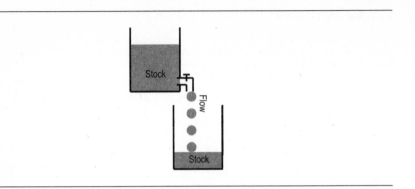

Figure 9.6   Simple Flow between Two Stocks

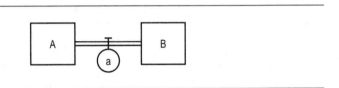

Figure 9.7   Generic Representation of Stocks and Flows

Each of the flows is controlled by formulae that can include the level of any stock as a variable. Figure 9.7 shows a more generic representation of the same concept, which lends itself more effectively to designing a simulation model.

To demonstrate how such a function can be used, consider again the production customer loyalty model of Figure 9.5. One of the first requests made of the system, based on the results of the prototype, is to list the customers for each store. Since the direct hierarchical relationship between the customer and store has been replaced by complex relationships (through updates, sales, and redemptions), this list has to be derived. A simple assumption could be made that the customer belongs to a given store based on the last record in each of the three joining entities (customer update, sale transaction, and points redemption) with conflicts resolved on numbers and ties arbitrated by a priority on customer update, sale transaction, and points redemption. These are arbitrary rules that could easily vary and serve to demonstrate the principles of simulation and unstable behavior. In effect, the three joining entities act as a force that sets customers in a form of orbit around stores. Some customers might enter a stable orbit, while others might move apparently freely between stores.

For the purposes of designing the business rules, as well as gaining a better insight into the business, a system dynamics model could be created for a three-store system. The stock in the system is the number of customers deemed to be associated with the store. For the purposes of the simulation, assume the parameters shown in Table 9.5.

The system dynamics model corresponding to this is shown in Figure 9.8.

The arrows joining the stocks to the flows provides for a feedback loop of some kind; that is, the number of customers assigned to a store will actually cause a change to the rate itself. In this diagram, *A, B,* and *C* correspond to the number of customers assigned to stores *A, B,* and *C*. While *a, b,* and *c* correspond to the rate of flow between each of the stores (a positive value flows in the direction of the arrow and a negative in the opposite).

For the purposes of illustration, the simulation was run with only the parameters described in Table 9.5 and no feedback loop. It would make sense to take the impact of larger stores on the movement of customers to gain further confidence on the stability or instability of the solution. Running the simulation one day at a time over 12 months, taking a snapshot at the end of each month, gave the results shown in Table 9.6. A quick examination shows that there is no long-term trend toward a stable allocation of customers per store and that the variation is of the order of plus or minus 25 percent, which would make any store/customer reporting using this model and the described business rules unacceptable.

Table 9.5 Simulation Parameters

Parameter	Value
Number of stores	3
Number of customers	120
Number of sales per customer	2 per month
Number of customer updates	2 per year (phone number, e-mail, address, and so on)
Number of points redemptions	2 per year
Trading days per month	25 (rounded for simplicity)
Distribution between stores	50% shop 90% at one store, 30% shop 75% at one store, and 20% shop 50% at one store (balance distributed evenly between the other two stores)
Initial state	40 customers assigned to each store

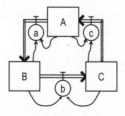

Figure 9.8 Simulation Model

Table 9.6 Simulation Results

	Customers Assigned per Store		
Month	Store A	Store B	Store C
Initial state	40	40	40
1	38	43	39
2	40	43	37
3	35	41	44
4	38	42	40
5	41	39	40
6	48	36	36
7	41	47	32
8	41	32	47
9	45	28	47
10	49	32	39
11	53	29	38
12	39	41	40

Further analysis would show whether fine-tuning the business rules caused dramatic changes (further indication of chaotic behavior when very small changes cause very large variations downstream) or could, more realistically, assign customers to a home store.

It is interesting to note that this relatively simple business scenario results in three forces acting on individual customers very much like the complexity associated with the three-body gravitational problem. As with other fields of science, the same underlying challenges and mathematical situations have a tendency to appear repeatedly.

DATA AS AN ALGORITHM

Information is both complex (as described in this chapter) and the result of processes (as described in Chapter 6). These two facts combined mean the practice of managing by a set of metrics is likely to lead to poor decisions being made. Metrics are the business form of equations, which in turn are defined as describing two algebraic expressions that are equal or equivalent.

$$Expression\ 1 = Expression\ 2$$

For example:

$$Return\ on\ Equity\ (ROE) = \frac{Net\ Income}{Average\ Stockholder\ Equity}$$

Consider each variable to be a stock in the sense of system dynamics. Each metric reflects the value of the stocks at the conclusion of individual instances of each business process. A good example of such a metric is performance to promise in supply chain:

$$Performance\ to\ Promise\ (supply\ chain) = \frac{Number\ of\ items\ delivered\ on\ time}{Total\ items\ ordered}$$

The metric is often used as part of the executive monthly scorecard. Further, the executive team may have demonstrated that there is a causal relationship between the performance to promise metric and customer satisfaction, which in turn has a causal relationship to revenue growth. As shown, the performance to promise metric is generally calculated as being the percentage of the order (by unit) that is delivered on time. If an order is received for four items, three of which are shipped by the agreed date, then the metric is 75 percent.

From a management perspective, this provides a digestible indication of business performance. Because it is calculated based on performance of orders, it is best described as a lag indicator. That is, the result lags the activity itself.

In order to manage the complexity of the enterprise, most scorecards that include this type of indicator also assume some type of relationship between staffing and stock levels, which can crudely improve the performance of the supply chain. Management then moves their various controls, such as staff rosters or available stock, or perhaps vary manufacturing capacity based on the performance of the metrics.

Equations that attempt to describe supply chains become mathematically complex and are much better understood as an algorithm rather than a disparate set of metrics. In Chapter 16, the MIT Beer Game will be introduced, which allows participants to see a particular example of how even apparently simple supply chain relationships quickly become complex.

An alternative approach to simply monitoring the individual metric is to look at the elements that make up performance to promise and treat them as an algorithm. If there were four steps in the algorithm, they might look something like:

1. Receive the order
2. Commit to a delivery date
3. Manufacture the product
4. Deliver the product

These can be divided into two distinct algorithms that determine the performance to promise result. The first is based on the setting of the promise (in steps one and two). The second is the meeting of that promise (in steps three and four). Understanding the first starts to tell executives something about the aggressiveness of the company in making a promise to customers. The second says something about the resourcing in materials and manpower.

In a classic business process reengineering exercise, both processes would be recalibrated to the business goals. Perhaps changing the first to make less ambitious promises where there is little to be gained in terms of customer goodwill (it is often better to promise a date that is a few days later, but always deliver on time). The reengineering might also change the second to better allocate resources in the manufacturing and fulfillment process. Treating the metric as an algorithm from the start has the potential to expose the entire process of calculation much earlier on to the executive team and provide a tool for a more granular level of decision making.

Rather than simply reporting the aggregate performance to promise, it is possible to observe the algorithm in motion by looking at its constituent parts. The calculation of a promise date could be described as a delivery time variable, assigned T. The manufacturing capacity might be assigned C, which is a function of staffing (S) and available materials (M):

$$C = fn(S, M)$$

The amount of time it takes to complete manufacturing depends on all of the outstanding orders that need to be produced by time T, referred to as O_T, which is in turn a function of capacity. The following four steps are a simple example of an algorithm that a business might choose to implement to determine the promise date:

1. How much capacity slack exists for each of the next n days (n representing half the average production time)?
2. Is that sufficient to process the order?
3. If not, double n and return to step 2.
4. If so, add the order into the system and update the forward load.

Altering the algorithm has a significant impact on the promise date, which in turn will impact the performance to promise metric. By understanding the algorithm rather than the end metric, business executives are empowered to directly tune the business in many more dimensions than simply reacting to a lag metric normally allows. An information system can interpret the algorithm, rather than simply aggregate the operational data to create a simple metric. Equipped with such a system, which provides data about every step in the algorithm, executives can see the range of business options available to tune the business to achieve the optimal performance to promise.

VIRTUAL MODELS AND INTEGRATION

Most approaches to providing information to support decision making, information retrieval, or simple reporting rely on some form of data duplication in the form of data warehouses, master data management services, document repositories, and similar architectures. It is regularly suggested both within industry and the vendor community that a virtual solution should be possible. In fact, there are often claims by some organizations that they have implemented exactly that type of solution.

In Chapter 10, an examination of the major data warehouse architectures is undertaken. However, for the purpose of understanding the virtual option, it is sufficient to identify that there are a number of requirements of an analytical solution for it to be complete, including time-series data (that is, it needs to provide extensive history) and integration across domains (that is, it shouldn't require that analysis or retrieval is done by an individual business unit or line). In some cases, the so-called virtual solution is nothing more than exposing of existing tables in a location that permits query, in which case, it isn't relevant. The more sophisticated virtual solution attempts to replicate the functionality of a true data warehouse or document repository.

The challenge that such a solution faces is dealing with the complexity of the data. In this sense, complexity is meant technically not generically. That is, this chapter has shown that data and models meet the criteria for complex and often chaotic mathematical systems. By definition, it is impossible to predict, in advance, any chaotic system's parameters, and this is particularly true of complex information.

A physical copy of the data provides the opportunity to synchronize the state of each subject and entity within the model, meeting many of the requirements to dampen chaotic behavior. Without the stable and controlled copy, the virtual solution is left trying to reconcile the different tables across many different databases, each of which has different frequencies of update, rules for reconciliation, and referential integrity requirements.

Without the physical copy, the chaotic attributes of the enterprise model cannot be tamed and it is practically and usually theoretically impossible to have a fully reconciled, historically consistent decision support and general information repository.

CHAOS OR COMPLEXITY

As a final note on this topic, it is worth remembering that the theory of chaos falls into the discipline of complexity. Broadly speaking, Chaos theory is about finding the parameters of systems, such as the one prototyped that cause unstable behavior. Unstable behavior is usually characterized by small changes in the initial conditions having a dramatic impact on the system in later cycles. More broadly, when people discuss Complexity theory, they are looking first for Weaver's organized complexity, which is about finding simple and stable states that emerge from complex systems. Some systems look, on the surface, to be extremely complex, but with the right configuration, actually generate highly predictable and stable results. Perhaps this reflects the well-known trait of humans to look for patterns in everything. We assume they are there before we begin to accept that the content may be unpredictable.

NOTES

1. W. Weaver (1948), "Science and Complexity," *American Scientist*, 36:536.

2. E. Lorenz (1987), *Chaos: Making a New Science* (New York: Viking Penguin Inc).

3. R. Hillard, P. Blecher, and P. O'Donnell (1999), "The Implications of Chaos Theory on the Management of a Data Warehouse," Proceedings of the International Society of Decision Support Systems (ISDSS).

4. R. R. Panko (January 2005), "What We Know about Spreadsheet Errors." Available at http://panko.cba.hawaii.edu/ssr/whatknow.htm.

Chapter 10

Comparing Data Warehouse Architectures

The architecture wars have raged for years about when and why different types of data warehouse solutions should get built. Some advocate an interventionist approach in which enterprise data warehouses are developed that are fundamental to the enterprise, while others recommend a softer touch with departmental business intelligence solutions and virtual integration of data sets.

All of the approaches have one thing in common: In some way, they duplicate at least the business rules and almost always the data associated with individual business application instances across the enterprise.

At first glance, this may appear counterintuitive. If the objective is to have a consistent view of business data, then duplicating the content introduces multiple opportunities for error. In addition, many senior technology executives are concerned about the cost of storage with ongoing duplication of content; much of this concern is due to their experiences as middle managers in the 1980s and 1990s when such storage was excessively expensive. The cost of storage should seldom be an issue today.

DATA WAREHOUSING

The data warehouse seems to have come into being without any single inventor, although system architects at Digital Equipment Corporation (DEC) and IBM both lay claim through the 1980s to early development of the concept. IBM in particular invested in the concept of a so-called "information warehouse" providing an integrated view of the enterprise.

Through the 1990s, the debate raged with two primary authors driving the discussion.

The first to market in 1991 was Bill Inmon, with the book *Building the Data Warehouse*,[1] who advocated a fully integrated store of information using the definition that a data warehouse is "a subject-oriented, integrated, time-variant, non-volatile collection of data used to support the strategic decision-making process for the enterprise."

The second, but equally influential, is Ralph Kimball, who published his book *The Data Warehouse Toolkit*[2] in 1996. Kimball takes the view that the task of designing an integrated enterprise model is unachievable and takes the pragmatic approach that the data warehouse is simply "a copy of transaction data specifically structured for query and analysis." Kimball, however, advocates a more substantial transformation of the content of the data model introducing readers to the concept of *dimensional modeling*.

The techniques of information entropy and the Small Worlds measures allow practitioners to understand the costs and benefits of the different techniques. With quantitative measures and common language, it becomes possible to tailor a solution to the business objectives of the enterprise.

CONTRASTING THE INMON AND KIMBALL APPROACHES

The Inmon approach to data warehousing is best described as being data driven, having everything integrated using the principles of normalization (typically third-normal form) as described in Chapter 4. In its simplest form, all queries are sourced from the same integrated model (as shown in Figure 10.1). The elegance of Inmon's approach is that the design approach is independent of the analysis of the decisions that are made using the data.

A successful Inmon Data Warehouse architecture will provide an integrated enterprise view of all relevant data held by the organization. Such an architecture will serve the business well for many years, with new requirements being easily sourced from within the enterprise repository.

In contrast, a typical Kimball Data Warehouse turns the data-driven approach on its head and is far more user driven, with the underlying data model tailored to the decisions that are known to be needed. Rather than leaving all data integrated, the Kimball approach breaks the enterprise model of Inmon into smaller dimensional models, a lightly denormalized form of the relational model.

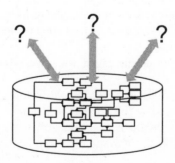

Figure 10.1   Typical Inmon Approach

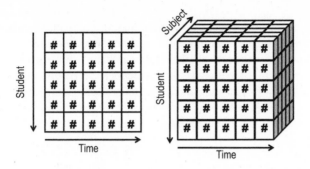

Figure 10.2   Two and Three Dimensions

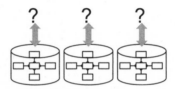

Figure 10.3   Typical Kimball Approach

Dimensional models are still standard relational models as defined by Codd, but they do not adhere to the third-normal form advocated by most modeling purists. Rather than require each relationship to be unique, dimensional models permit and encourage duplication for the aid of usage.

Kimball invented the term *conformed dimension* to describe a standard easy-to-use technique for navigating the model (solving the average degree problem facing the Inmon approach). Visualizing data in two, three, and many dimensions, Kimball uses conformed dimensions to allow users to navigate quickly to a numeric "fact." Each fact is simply a metric at the intersection of two or more dimensions as shown in Figure 10.2.

The architecture of a Kimball-style data warehouse can be stylized as shown in Figure 10.3, with each user requirement sourced from a dedicated model fragment.

QUANTITY IMPLICATIONS

The two approaches both source their data from the same operational business systems. However, the resulting quantity of data is quite different. The reason is easily seen using the concept of information entropy that was introduced in Chapter 6.

To illustrate the difference, consider an organization with 10 customers (Anne, Brian, Charles, Dianne, Edward, Fiona, Graeme, Harry, Isabella, and John). In an Inmon-style data warehouse, all the customer data would be contained in one database table. In a Kimball-style data warehouse, the customer data would be distributed to tables that are relevant to the individual decision makers. In the real world, this might align to the situation where there are multiple divisions who look after the different groups of customers.

Inmon Style	Kimball Style	
Anne	Anne	Fiona
Brian	Brian	Graeme
Charles	Charles	Harry
Dianne	Dianne	Isabella
Edward	Edward	John
Fiona		
Graeme		
Harry		
Isabella		
John		

Let's consider the information entropy of these two situations. Remember from Chapter 6 that the information entropy (H) of each record is calculated by:

$$H = -\sum_{i=1}^{n} p(x_i) log_2 \, p(x_i)$$

Where n is the number of states that an individual record could represent, x_i represents each of those potential states, and $p(x_i)$ represents the probability that an individual record holds an individual value x_i.

In the Inmon example, there is one table that combines all 10 customers. Each record in the database has 10 potential values so the probability of a record holding any one of them is $\frac{1}{10}$ or 0.1. The entropy of an individual record is therefore:

$$H = -\sum_{i=1}^{10} \frac{1}{10} log_2 \frac{1}{10} = log_2 10 = 3.32$$

With 10 rows in the table the information entropy of this example is $10 log_2 10 = 33.22$ (as a hint, $log_2 10 = -log_2 \frac{1}{10}$)

In the case of the Kimball example, there are five potential values in the first table (Anne, Brian, Charles, Dianne, or Edward) and the probability of a record holding any one of them is therefore $\frac{1}{5}$ or 0.2. The entropy of an individual record is therefore:

$$H = -\sum_{i=1}^{5} \frac{1}{5} log_2 \frac{1}{5} = log_2 5 = 2.32$$

As there are five rows in the first table of this Kimball example that can have any of these five values (Anne, Brian, Charles, Dianne and Edward), then the information entropy of the first table is $5log_2 5 = 11.61$ and since there are two tables with the same number of rows and potential customers, the total entropy of the example is $5log_2 5 + 5log_2 5 = 23.22$.

The interpretation of this analysis is that an Inmon-style data warehouse provides a higher level of information for decision making than siloed and unintegrated individual stores of the Kimball approach. Without necessarily focusing on the mathematical foundations, Bill Inmon has long advocated an approach that maximizes the information value and information entropy.

USABILITY IMPLICATIONS

Recall the example of the parent, student, teacher model, also from Chapter 4. Consider now the next logical extension of the model, the addition of marks for each student's subject work as shown in Figure 10.4.

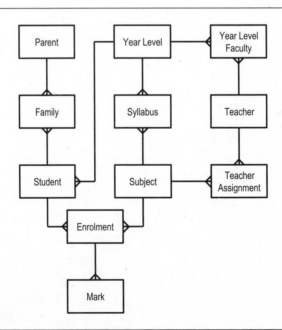

Figure 10.4   School Entity Relationship Model with Marks

The concept of subject marks has been added to the student-subject enrollment (which acts as a many-to-many resolver for the two entities). Each student receives multiple marks for each subject enrollment.

This model represents a good example of an integrated data model that would be well regarded by advocates of the Inman approach to data warehousing. However, a review of the Small Worlds measure shows the extent of the problem. Recall the technique as outlined in Chapter 5. The first step is to generalize the model to a graph as shown in Figure 10.5.

With this generic view, the degree and geodesic distances can be calculated as shown in Table 10.1.

The average degree is 2.2, the maximum geodesic distance is 5, and the average geodesic distance is 2.4. Based on the analysis described in Chapter 5, the average degree is a problem, as there are between two and three options from every entity, creating ambiguity. In addition, for a model of only 11 entities, to have a maximum geodesic distance of five indicates that there are already elements of the model that would be unusable by most people.

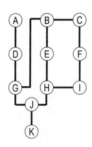

Figure 10.5 Graph Representing School ER Model

Table 10.1 Degree and Geodesic Distance

V	D			A	B	C	D	E	F	G	H	I	J	K
A	1		A		2	4	1	4	5	2	4	5	3	4
B	3		B	2		1	2	1	2	1	2	3	2	3
C	2		C	4	1		3	2	1	2	3	2	3	4
D	2		D	1	2	3		2	4	1	3	4	2	3
E	2		E	4	1	2	2		3	2	1	2	2	3
F	2		F	5	2	1	4	3		3	2	1	3	4
G	3		G	2	1	2	1	2	3		2	3	1	2
H	3		H	4	2	3	3	1	2	2		1	1	2
I	2		I	5	3	2	4	2	1	3	1		2	3
J	3		J	3	2	3	2	2	3	1	1	2		1
K	1		K	4	3	4	3	3	4	2	2	3	1	

The Kimball approach to the same problem would look at student marks as the metric or "fact." An individual mark is meaningful when combined with a time (for instance, there might be a January and June mark issued). A unique mark can be accessed by combining time, student, and subject together (three dimensions as shown in the cube).

A fact, however, does not need to be viewed individually—it can be aggregated in some way. In the case of a mark, it should be averaged. If marks are out of 100, then the aggregate of a set of three marks {60, 80, 90} is the average: 76.7. Other facts, such as sales figures are aggregated by summing them; for instance, the aggregate of {$600, $800, $900} is the sum: $2,300.

In the school example, the combination of student and time (shown in the two-dimensional cube in Figure 10.2) would be the average of marks across all of the subjects taken by the student. Similarly, it would make sense to analyze teacher performance by subject (comparing one teacher's marks to another taking the same subject).

The way that a dimensional model is defined is still by using entity-relationship diagrams; however, there is no attempt to maintain the same level of normalization and the tables are divided into facts and dimensions as shown in Figure 10.6.

The degree and geodesic distances of the dimensional view can be calculated as shown using Figure 10.7 and Table 10.2.

The dimensional approach results in an average degree of 1.6, average geodesic distance also of 1.6, and a maximum geodesic distance of just 2. Across all of the

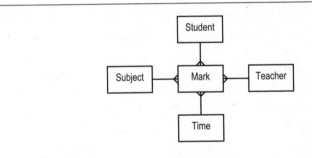

Figure 10.6 Dimensional Version of School Model

Table 10.2 Degree and Geodesic Distance

V	D			A	B	C	D	E
A	1		A		2	1	2	2
B	1		B	2		1	2	2
C	4		C	1	1		1	1
D	1		D	2	2	1		2
E	1		E	2	2	1	2	

Figure 10.7   Graph Representing the Dimensional Model

Small Worlds metrics, the Kimball-style model is a much more usable solution but it has lost information (quantity) in the process.

To understand how much information has been lost, the entities need to be populated in a worked example. Consider a scenario in which there are five students {Andrew, Betty, Charles, Dianne, Edward} who are enrolled in four subjects {English, Mathematics, Physics, Art} taken by five teachers {Ms. Fisher, Mr. Gill, Ms. Harris, Mr. Innes, Ms. Johnson}. Each subject is awarded two marks {mid-term, end-term}. In this scenario, there are four dimension tables. Note that the term *PK* refers to the primary key (a numeric surrogate).

PK	Student	PK	Subject	PK	Teacher	PK	Time
1	Andrew	1	English	1	Ms. Fisher	1	Mid-term
2	Betty	2	Mathematics	2	Mr. Gill	2	End-term
3	Charles	3	Physics	3	Ms. Harris		
4	Dianne	4	Art	4	Mr. Innes		
5	Edward			5	Ms. Johnson		

The combined raw data, with marks out of 100, is shown in the following table:

Student	Subject	Teacher	Time	Mark
Andrew	English	Ms. Fisher	Mid-term	75
Andrew	English	Ms. Fisher	End-term	80
Andrew	Mathematics	Mr. Gill	Mid-term	45
Andrew	Mathematics	Mr. Gill	End-term	50
Andrew	Physics	Ms. Harris	Mid-term	40
Andrew	Physics	Ms. Harris	End-term	45
Betty	English	Mr. Innes	Mid-term	60
Betty	English	Mr. Innes	End-term	55
Betty	Mathematics	Mr. Gill	Mid-term	65
Betty	Mathematics	Mr. Gill	End-term	70
Betty	Art	Ms. Johnson	Mid-term	90
Betty	Art	Ms. Johnson	End-term	90
Charles	English	Ms. Fisher	Mid-term	80

continued

Student	Subject	Teacher	Time	Mark
Charles	English	Ms. Fisher	End-term	45
Charles	Physics	Mr. Gill	Mid-term	85
Charles	Physics	Mr. Gill	End-term	60
Charles	Art	Ms. Fisher	Mid-term	95
Charles	Art	Ms. Fisher	End-term	75
Dianne	English	Ms. Fisher	Mid-term	50
Dianne	English	Ms. Fisher	End-term	80
Dianne	Mathematics	Mr. Gill	Mid-term	60
Dianne	Mathematics	Mr. Gill	End-term	70
Dianne	Physics	Ms. Harris	Mid-term	70
Dianne	Physics	Ms. Harris	End-term	75
Edward	Mathematics	Ms. Harris	Mid-term	80
Edward	Mathematics	Ms. Harris	End-term	90
Edward	Physics	Mr. Gill	Mid-term	65
Edward	Physics	Mr. Gill	End-term	60
Edward	Art	Ms. Johnson	Mid-term	50
Edward	Art	Ms. Johnson	End-term	55

This content is converted into a fact table in the following structure. The foreign keys are a link back to the primary keys of the dimension tables. The primary key of the fact table is the combination of its foreign keys.

Student	Subject	Teacher	Time	Mark
1	1	1	1	75
1	1	1	2	80
1	2	2	1	45
1	2	2	2	50
1	3	3	1	40
1	3	3	2	45
2	1	4	1	60
2	1	4	2	55
2	2	2	1	65
2	2	2	2	70
2	4	5	1	90
2	4	5	2	90
3	1	1	1	80
3	1	1	2	45
3	3	2	1	85
3	3	2	2	60
3	4	1	1	95
3	4	1	2	75
4	1	1	1	50
4	1	1	2	80
4	2	2	1	60
4	2	2	2	70

continued

| Foreign Keys | | | | |
Student	Subject	Teacher	Time	Mark
4	3	3	1	70
4	3	3	2	75
5	2	3	1	80
5	2	3	2	90
5	3	2	1	65
5	3	2	2	60
5	4	5	1	50
5	4	5	2	55

The dimensional view of the school model is much easier to understand for the novice user, but it also loses subtle information such as the relationships between teachers, subjects, students, and families. Of course, much of this can be inferred, which is the argument used by dimensional model advocates.

How much data is lost is best understood by comparing the information entropy of the dimensional school model. The dimensional model information entropy is calculated by the sum of the entropy of each entity:

$$students + subjects + teachers + time + marks$$

Each individual entropy value is determined by the number of rows and the values that are permitted for each row. For simplicity, it is assumed that all marks are equal (although it would be technically correct to distribute on a bell curve):

$$5 log_2 5 + 4 log_2 4 + 5 log_2 5 + 2 log_2 2 + 30 log_2 100 = 232.5 \, bits$$

The information entropy of the normalized model is calculated by summing the individual entities. The equivalent entities are shown in Figure 10.8. For the purposes of this simplified analysis, parents and family concepts have been removed. While the parents and family concepts could be represented in a special dimensional structure called a *snowflake*, even more information would be lost in the process.

The information entropy is calculated as the sum of the entities (again using the simplifying assumption that the relationships are evenly distributed):

$$Student + Subject + Teacher + Enrollment + Teacher \, Assignment + Mark$$

Student, Subject, Teacher, and *Mark* are the same in both the dimensional and normalized cases. However, the addition of *Enrollment* and *Teacher Assignment* reflects additional information. *Enrollment* resolves *Students* and *Subjects* while

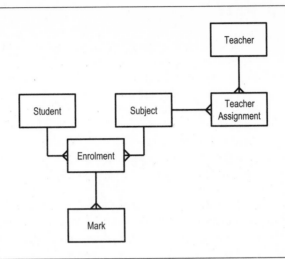

Figure 10.8   Normalized Equivalent Model

Teacher Assignment resolves *Teachers* and *Subjects*. Each has two fields that have permissible values up to the population of the parent entity; the population of the resolver is the product of the population of both parent entities.

  Enrollment has two parents: *Student* (with a population of 5) and *Subject* (with a population of 4). As a result, the two fields have an entropy of $log_2 5$ and $log_2 4$, respectively. There could be up to 4×5 (20) unique combinations that provide the total potential population; hence, the information entropy of *Enrollment* is:

$$20(log_2 5 + log_2 4) = 86.4$$

  Similarly, *Teacher Assignment* has two parents: *Teacher* (with a population of 5) and *Subject* (with a population of 4), again giving two field entropies of $log_2 5$ and $log_2 4$, respectively, with the same number of combinations (20) and a total information entropy also of 86.4. The total information entropy of Figure 10.8 is then calculated to be:

$$5\,log_2 5 + 4\,log_2 4 + 5\,log_2 5 + 2\,log_2 2 + 30\,log_2 100$$
$$+ 20(log_2 5 + log_2 4) + 20(log_2 5 + log_2 4) = 405.4$$

  In summary, even this simple dimensional and normalized model example shows that while the dimensional form is much easier to understand, more than 40 percent of the information content is lost.

HISTORICAL DATA

One problem that all data warehouse strategies have to tackle is the management of historical data. Historical data comes in many forms. The simplest type of history is the posting of transactions over time, such as sales records, purchase orders, or manufacturing runs. More complicated are the changes to reference data and master data that can be interpreted in a multitude of legitimate ways.

The decision about what to do with transaction data varies according to the architecture chosen and the business rules selected on data retention. With constantly decreasing storage costs, many organizations are simply electing to keep all transactions online indefinitely. This is not as irresponsible or radical as it might sound, at first.

For instance, imagine a supermarket chain that takes in $10 billion per year. Assume the average product costs $1; then that equates to 10 billion individual product sales (the most granular level of detail). Further, imagine that each transaction requires 100 bytes to fully describe it (a generous allocation). Each year the transaction file will require:

$$10 \text{ billion} \times 100 \text{ bytes} = 1000 \text{ Gigabyte} = 1 \text{ Terabyte}$$

One terabyte of storage is neither expensive nor complex to manage. By the time the years have accumulated, then the accumulated Moore's Law is likely to make 10 or 20 terabytes trivial as well.

The only nagging question is how to handle adjustments to history. Take, for instance, a transaction that is entered in error and is later reversed. It would be better for sales analysis if the transaction was never included. However, there is a possibility that it has been included in past transactions and it is necessary, to meet the nonvolatile condition of Inmon's data warehouse definition, to be able to replicate such a report at any time in the future.

The simple solution is to ensure every transaction has both a transaction time and a posting time. The transaction time records the time that the event is allocated to, and the posting time records the time that it was received into the data warehouse. Reporting layers can make the decision about whether to include or exclude later posted corrections in a given report based on the business requirement (usually deciding whether to duplicate an earlier report or provide the most accurate view of business data available).

Reference data, or data that is used to navigate and parameterize questions, is significantly more complex. For instance, a structural change to the organization's management hierarchy could reallocate sales, people, or products between reporting groups. In some situations, all historical reporting, when reprinted, needs to be in the new hierarchy to support like-for-like comparisons. In other situations, the user may seek to replicate reporting that was produced in the past.

In the Inmon architecture, this problem is largely seen as belonging to the report writer, providing that the underlying data model provides the capability, consistent with the rules of Third Normal Form modeling, to either extract the current hierarchy or the historical hierarchy.

In the Kimball architecture, the dimensional models are intended to anticipate the user requirements. This effectively means that different dimensional structures are required for both scenarios. The handling of these changes, called *slowly changing dimensions*, is described in Chapter 12.

Data warehouse designers need to make complex decisions about the handling of history. While it is ideal to provide all historical changes in anticipation of every required scenario, it is usually not possible. For instance, on a customer record, re-creating minor changes such as a correction to postal code may not be relevant and could cause a great deal of model complexity. At the very least, however, data warehouse modelers should allow for a change audit trail, which is a simple entity or group of entities that record all changes in a log. The log can be as simple as a table code (from the metadata) indicating which table had the change applied, an attribute code (also from the metadata), a copy of the old and new attribute values together with the times that the change occurred and was posted. Such a log is not useful for reporting or analysis; however, it is ideal for forensic analysis when something has gone wrong such as fraud or even simply system issues.

SUMMARY

The debate on whether to use a Kimball-style dimensional architecture or to build an Inmon-style enterprise data warehouse has long been based on the individual experiences of the practitioner. As described in Chapter 1, different corporate strategic objectives should drive different styles of information management. This chapter has described techniques for quantifying the trade-off between the two most common analytical architectures.

Businesses that are striving to maximize the use of complex information and hence are willing to trade-off content for usability can use these techniques to quantify the amount of information that they are prepared to use. In contrast, those organizations that are seeking to extract every ounce of value from the information that they hold now have a clear quantitative reason to go with an Inmon-style architecture.

Regardless of the business objectives, the information entropy and Small Worlds measures both clearly show that there is substantial value and necessity in following at least one of the recognized data warehouse architectures.

The message of this analysis is clear. Organizations have three options:

Option 1. Build an Inmon-style data warehouse that maximizes the value of the information (measured through the information entropy) with some compromise to the accessibility and usability (measured through the Small Worlds metrics).

Option 2. Build a Kimball-style data warehouse that maximizes the accessibility and usability (measured through the Small Worlds metrics) with some compromise to the value of the information (measured through the information entropy).

Option 3. Do nothing, leaving the data tied up in operational systems, and suffer poor information value (measured through the information entropy) and poor usability (measured through the Small Worlds metrics).

NOTES

1. W. H. Inmon (1991), *Building the Data Warehouse* (Hoboken, NJ: John Wiley & Sons, Inc.).
2. R. Kimball (1996), *The Data Warehouse Toolkit* (Hoboken, NJ: John Wiley & Sons, Inc.).

Chapter 11

Layered View of Information

Despite the arguments about the best technical architecture to provide information to the business, almost every organization has a number of things in common. First, most have a management structure split into nonexecutive supervisors (usually a board), an executive team, and an army of middle managers. Second, they have an enormous appetite for complex data at every level. Finally, in every industry sector, there is terminology that defines activity and success.

Consider the two extremes of business.

At the top of the management tree are a group of executives. Each has a short tenure, often less than two years. During that time, they need to streamline the information they have to achieve an agenda or incorporate change.

At the bottom or foundation of the enterprise are the operational processes, systems, and people who make the business run. These processes and systems are rich in raw data. Data is highly denormalized; that is, there are many duplications of content and little integration across business processes.

Between these two extremes sits an army of middle managers who spend vast amounts of time responding to the executive requests for information by mapping the operational data into metrics.

Every enterprise, and in particular every leader, has a preferred strategy for tackling the challenges that the market, stakeholders, or the sector creates. This strategy needs to be measured in terms that a board or executive leadership can understand and support. These measures are usually straightforward metrics. Some examples include concepts like unit gross margins, resource utilization, and return on equity. The metrics used to drive the business change rapidly as both the leadership and organizational strategies evolve.

Because of the rushed nature of the requests made by executives for data (after all, they have only a small window of opportunity to demonstrate their success) few quality controls are put in place along the way. The lack of controls is despite the move to greater financial and process regulation worldwide in almost every aspect of business and government, since these controls have almost exclusively been applied to operational activities of the enterprise.

While the tenure of the executive team is usually short, the ranks of middle management usually include a substantial body of staff who have been in place for an extended period of time and have considerable corporate memory. These staff are usually frustrated by the requests for the same data by generation after generation of executive management with small differences between the requirements.

Similarly, they are frustrated that there is usually little appetite to put in place a more strategic framework to provide this content.

INFORMATION LAYERS

At a logical level, the enterprise has four layers of information. At the top and bottom, as already described, are the metrics and operational data, respectively. To make sense of the operational data, there has to be a layer of normalization; it is simply the only abstract tool available that integrates and describes data in atomic terms.

For all the reasons that we've described, it is difficult to interpret a normalized model. The natural tendency is to create dimensions and formally or informally define a dimensional model. Such a view of the enterprise sits between the normalized and metric layers of the enterprise.

Considered together, the four layers can be visualized as a pyramid as shown in Figure 11.1. Of course, without a proper architecture, the picture looks more like Figure 11.2, with each layer of integration requiring substantial manual effort using spreadsheets and other tools.

Each layer of information has its own characteristics. Metrics are easily digestible, dimensions allow for intuitive navigation, normalized data holds the key to the riches of data mining, and operational data is inherently tied to business processes.

Metrics are dependent on both the organizational structure and the strategy of the business while both are changing rapidly. This is because the executives defining the strategy and hence the metrics have a high rate of turnover. The dependency on the organization structure is due to divisional reporting requirements.

The dimensional view streamlines products and divisions into consistent conformed dimensions; however, the particular schemas that are defined are dependent

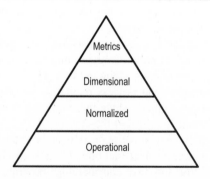

Figure 11.1   Layers of Information

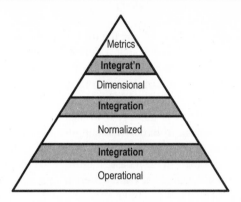

Figure 11.2   Layers with Manual Integration

on the metrics that are required, hence the strategy of the day. As a result, the dimensional view also changes rapidly. Given that the organizational structure usually changes marginally more often than the corporate strategy, the dimensional view is slightly more stable than the metric view.

The principles of third-normal form modeling mean that the normalized view of the enterprise should be independent of both strategy and organization structure.

The normalized model should describe the fundamental business data as generated by the underlying business processes and not be biased toward the information that is required for analysis. For this reason, the normalized view that develops over time should be very stable.

The operational data is geared toward front-end systems that are operated within individual departments or divisions, hence is highly dependent on the organizational structure as well as the current business strategy. As a result, the operational layer changes as often as the metrics layer. Given the length of time it takes to implement most complex business systems, it is not surprising that so many are supported by shadow systems or have fields that have been applied in ways that weren't originally intended.

ARE THEY REAL?

The layered view of enterprise data is not only an idealized approach but it also reflects the reality for almost all organizations. In most cases, however, these layers exist in an informal, virtual, or ad-hoc manner.

The first step to understanding why this is the case is to examine the transitions from the operational to the dimensional view and from the normalized model to the enterprise metrics—in each case, skipping the normalized or dimensional views, respectively.

In the first case, we'll attempt to make the transition of data from an operational view to the dimensional view. Recall that a dimensional model consists of a fact table linked to multiple conformed (i.e., consistent) dimension tables. The conformed dimension tables can, in turn, link to further fact tables.

Consider a manufacturing supply system, which is divided into internal and external supply. That is, the parts that are manufactured within other members of the group versus parts coming from external suppliers, as shown in Figure 11.3.

The internal stock transfers are handled by one system while the external purchases are handled by another. In each case, there is a list of parts, shipping dates, and quantities. Naturally, because they are different systems, the data looks quite different. For the sake of a simple example, assume that the only difference between the two systems is that, for internal stock movements, parts are described using an internal code, while external purchases are used using an industry standard code. The assembly system (a third system) contains a mapping from the external code to the internal code as shown in Figure 11.4.

A dimensional model that provides simple information about part availability would want to track estimated stock-on-hand based on current and future orders as shown in Figure 11.5.

The part register would provide an amount of existing stock using internal part codes, the internal stock transfers system would indicate the amount of stock that is due to arrive (again using internal part codes), and the external purchasing system would provide similar information, but this time using the industry part codes.

In the first instance, you might consider the conversion to be trivial with a simple one-for-one mapping—perhaps external code could even be an attribute of the internal part dimension. The translation requires a small amount of mental gymnastics, but nothing that couldn't be computed without resorting to an intermediary database.

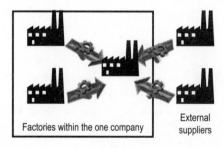

Factories within the one company

External suppliers

Figure 11.3 Flow of Parts

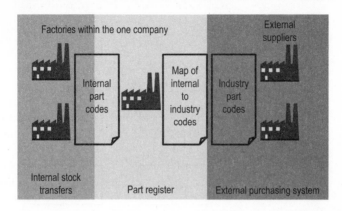

Figure 11.4   Part Codes

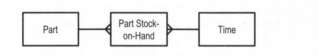

Figure 11.5   Simple Dimensional View

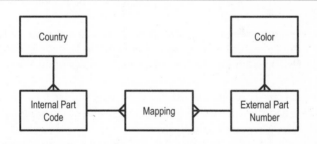

Figure 11.6   Mapping

However, such a mapping rarely exists. If it did, then the different systems would have adopted the same coding system. It has to be assumed that one internal part code could refer to more than one industry part number. Perhaps color doesn't matter internally, but externally red, green, and blue are coded differently. Similarly, one external part number could refer to more than one internal part code, perhaps referring to the country of origin (possibly required for regulatory requirements). The mapping might look something like Figure 11.6.

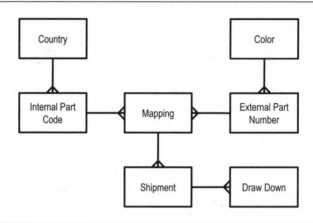

Figure 11.7   Normalized Model of Shipments

Such a mapping is still sufficiently simple that it could be completed by the use of in-memory variables during an extract, transform, and load process (commonly referred to as ETL). However, that doesn't change the fact that the in-memory transformation is effectively representing the data in a normalized form. As has already been shown, small additions to the logic and interfaces to other business processes will mean that the transformation model becomes increasingly complex, reaching a point rapidly where it needs to be implemented as a physical database. Regardless of whether this data is held permanently, it is in some way normalized before becoming dimensional.

Consider now the second transformation, from a normalized model through to the metrics. Again, consider the same business problem, but this time the stock-on-hand data has been represented in an extended normalized model shown in Figure 11.7.

Two new concepts have been added: the individual shipment that represents the amount of stock and the draw down on each shipment (which would also connect to the manufacturing process model).

We can imagine various metrics that an executive would want to see, but imagine a simple metric that indicated the quantity of parts at a point of time compared to the average over time:

$$\frac{Total\ unit\ quantity\ of\ parts}{Total\ average\ unit\ quantity\ of\ parts}$$

The first step would be to get a quantity on hand for each part at each point in time (perhaps for simplicity an end-of-month position would be appropriate). This could be represented as a table derived from the aggregate of each part's shipments and draw down.

Part Number	Month	Quantity on Hand
1	January 2008	43
1	February 2008	27
1	March 2008	35
2	January 2008	40
2	February 2008	39
2	March 2008	45
3	January 2008	20
3	February 2008	25
3	March 2008	29

From this simple list the average number of parts on hand in any given month is 101. The parts on hand in March 2008 was 109, which means that the metric of aggregate parts to average parts is:

$$\frac{109}{101} = 1.08$$

A closer examination of the table shows that it is in the same form as a dimensional analysis as shown in Figure 11.5. Again, it could be argued that this model could be implemented as an in-memory process during the ETL process that creates the metric, but it doesn't take much imagination to see that the addition of just one or two further dimensions will extend the complexity of this transformation beyond the capacity of even the most powerful machine.

Further, most executives when presented with a metric such as this one will follow up with questions about the breakdown. If the result of 1.08 is not acceptable, then the executive might wish to see a breakdown by part, which would require middle managers to again repeat the calculation, extracting the next level of granularity. More likely, they will anticipate the next requirement and store the dimensional result in a spreadsheet.

Regardless of whether the dimensional results are kept for a period or transitory, it is almost always necessary, as it was in this example, to create a dimensional view of normalized data in order to create a metric.

TURNING THE LAYERS INTO AN ARCHITECTURE

The astute reader will note a potential inconsistency in this analysis. In earlier chapters, we've identified the difficulty if not impossibility of creating a single integrated and normalized enterprise data model. The important thing to note is that in this chapter we have required only that a normalized model be created, not that it be complete or that it be fully integrated. Our analysis of information potential has shown that the more thoroughly the model is integrated, the greater the potential value of the content. However this should be an evolutionary goal rather than an up-front requirement.

In previous chapters, we've identified the important role that an Enterprise Metadata model should play. With the information layers identified we can now establish an Enterprise Metadata model, which links each of these layers together.

Figure 11.8 shows how the layers of information can be glued together if they're properly supported by a Metadata model and are highly integrated with visualization and analysis tools.

Like the layers themselves, the Metadata model is highly customized to the enterprise. There are, however, some elements that tend to repeat from organization to organization. The model itself is linked at all four layers describing the underlying elements as shown in Figure 11.9.

This underlying Metadata model provides linkage between each of the layers, at the same time providing the capacity for seamless user access to information at every level of data. With defined relationships between the layers, the need for manual manipulation and translation by middle managers is greatly reduced. Similarly, the opportunity for error is greatly reduced.

In defining the Metadata model for each of the layers, decisions need to also be made on the handling of history and, in particular, changes to definitions over time. At each layer, the decision about their handling may well be different.

In *operational* systems, the decision may be made that the systems are generally responsible for managing current data within the context of the definitions that are in place at that specific point in time.

In the *normalized* model, it is usual to support any change to master data, reference data, relationships, or definitions without compromise. Because of this requirement, most normalized models rapidly become quite complex.

In the *dimensional* layer, a more circumspect approach is normally taken to managing changes to dimensions, often called *slowly changing dimensions*. A

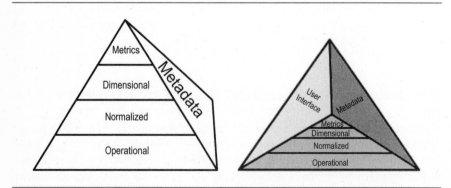

Figure 11.8   The Three Faces of the Organizational Architecture (front view and top view)

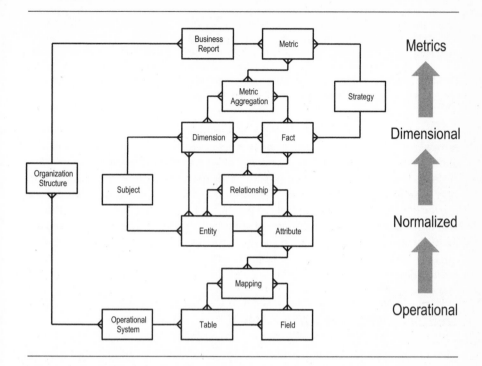

Figure 11.9   Example Metadata Model

decision is made on a case-by-case basis as to whether a change to a dimension table should be applied across all history or whether a separate row should be created to allow past facts to be recorded using the original definition.

In the *metrics* layer, it is normal to completely recast the metrics based on changes with little regard being made for history. This is usually acceptable and even desirable given the use of metrics to support executive decision making that needs to be simplified to provide clarity.

THE USER INTERFACE

In Chapter 8, we described the use of the Metadata model as a tool for navigating the enterprise. The Metadata model, described in Figure 11.9, is a subset of such an Enterprise Metadata model and supports a *verb-and-noun* approach to navigation.

Many software companies provide technology that allows for the aggregation of metrics, dimensional analysis, and at least some free-form queries against normalized tables. The key factors that technology departments should consider are:

User Interface	The software should be easy to use for business users, ideally consistent with other desktop tools they are used to.
Metadata	The user needs to be able to import, or even better use directly, external metadata. The Metadata model should not be overly restrictive.
Database support	Multiple relational database technologies should be supported because each layer may use more than one platform.

For many users, they will generally just use prepackaged queries and metrics; however, all staff are potentially going to want access to build new metrics, models, and queries from time to time—usually with an urgent deadline in mind.

As is usually the case with information management solutions, technology plays only a small role in the solution. Those individuals who are responsible for its implementation need to ensure that the purchase of software uses only a small fraction of the available budget. Even more important, they have to garner support from every level of the business to be actively involved in the implementation and ongoing governance of decision support systems that use the four layers of information.

SELLING THE ARCHITECTURE

Middle managers are generally frustrated by the amount of work that they have to undertake to provide short-term metrics for new executive management. Attempts to promote more sustainable solutions and correct errors that permeate enterprise decision making are often met with an executive response that "now is not the right time" and that "you have to survive the short term to be part of the long term." It is important to remember that the executive generally has a short tenure and little appetite for anything that he or she sees as requiring a longer attention span.

Ironically, there is another group who is both more senior and more likely to be a willing sponsor—the board, or in the case of public organizations, the political executive. These senior stakeholders usually have a longer tenure than the executive team. They also are in the position of having a greater legal accountability.

Often a leadership team is put in place based on their plans to implement a clean set of metrics to describe the business to investors. The board is ultimately accountable for the quality of information that is provided to investors and it is entirely possible that errors, ignored by the executive team, could result in an investor lawsuit in future years when problems emerge or a middle manager blows the whistle.

Because nonexecutive boards are usually drawn from the ranks of retired corporate leaders, their experience generally predates the information revolution and they have little understanding of the volume of data that is flowing around the enterprise. Often, they assume that standard audit processes are enough to guarantee that they are meeting their diligence obligations. However, a quick analysis of the information used by investors or, in the case of public agencies, the public shows that they rely increasingly on sophisticated measures that are drawn from nonledger sources deep inside the business.

The argument for implementing the architecture is made stronger by the reality that the layers exist anyway. Data is being created by virtue of temporary processes that simply need to be discovered and the content recorded. As a first step, this at least provides a more robust audit trail that the nonexecutive leadership team can look back to in the event of future problems. Further, it provides a baseline that can be used to support the transition between executive teams.

Having launched a pincer movement on the executive team from below and above, a virtue can be created of the necessity by rapidly providing decision support systems that allow for the follow-up questioning that has not previously been possible.

During the first implementations, it is important to remember that the role of the architecture is to record data that is already being created rather than try to solve every content problem at once. It is far more valuable to have content with a known level of accuracy than it is to have a data set of a higher quality but for which that level of quality is not understood. By simply encoding in databases data that is being created in spreadsheets, the organization is gaining an enormous amount of protection and opening the door to productivity improvements as teams begin to share complex data management processes.

Further, new business opportunities to package and sell data in different forms often manifest themselves. In almost every business, where there is complex data, there is a third party who can make effective use of that content. Strategists should look beyond customer data when considering third-party interest in data sets that the organization generates. Suppliers with complex supply chain processes can extract greater efficiencies if they have more accurate demand metrics. Retailers with shelf space can sell advertising and other facilities for a greater price if they can demonstrate better targeting of demographics. Financial institutions can better share risk if their partners can gain real-time information about facilities under threat of default.

Chapter 12

Master Data Management

Reference data can be thought of as nouns. A list of staff, customer, assets, or locations are all good examples of reference data. Recall that we can navigate data by *dimensions* (as shown visually in Figure 12.1), which is simply another term for reference data.

Ralph Kimball introduced the concept of *conformed dimensions*, referring to reference data sets that are common across dimensional models. For example, locations should be consistent across all analysis. In fact, the term *conformed dimension* is just a subset of another term: *master data*.

Master data is reference data that applies across systems, divisions, and departments. In other words, master data is enterprise reference data. A conformed dimension is master data applied to just one of the four information layers described in Chapter 11. Figure 12.2 shows how master data and conformed data map to the four layers of Chapter 11.

Because master data makes it much easier to generate conformed dimensions, it is sometimes stated that master data solutions remove or reduce the need for data warehouses. Master data solves many of the problems faced by complex organizations and makes it much easier to achieve the objectives of the four information layers described in Chapter 11.

Master data management is emerging as a practical approach to data integration. In some ways, it is a combination of an operational data store (providing an operational view of strategic data) as well as a slimmed-down data warehouse (avoiding many of the pitfalls of the enterprise data model described in Chapter 7).

PUBLISH AND SUBSCRIBE

Arguably, every process and system must use reference data of some form, and for it to be integrated with the wider organization, it must use master data (remembering that master data is defined as shared reference data).

Systems exist at all four information layers and sometimes support two or more tiers. While the definition of reference and master is quite simple, it is seldom as simply instantiated within real systems. The first task of any analysis is to identify the reference and master data used by each system and to do a Create-Read-Update-Delete (CRUD) matrix, which represents the facets of publishing and subscribing to master data.

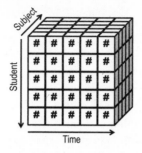

Figure 12.1 Navigating by Dimensions

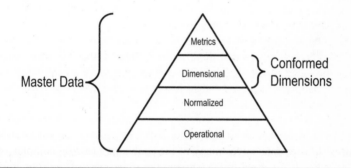

Figure 12.2 Master Data versus Conformed Dimensions

System: Point of Sale

	Create	Read	Update	Delete
Customer	✓	✓	✓	✓
Staff		✓		
Product		✓	✓	
Location		✓		

In this example, we can imagine a "smart" cash register that allows for the management of customer details, including their complete deletion upon request. Staff and location details can only be read, however, if there is the opportunity for corrections (i.e., updates) to be made to product information.

In an ideal architecture, each master data item would have only one point of creation, update, and deletion avoiding problems of synchronization across the network. The reality, however, is different with multiple systems needing to add and update entries on-the-fly. Of course, reading should never cause a significant problem.

ABOUT TIME

Designers of decision support systems (DSS), such as data warehouses, are familiar with the concept of modeling time. An enterprise approach to master data management should also start from the perspective of understanding the granularity of time. By establishing a timeline for the enterprise, synchronization becomes much easier.

The first facet of time that needs to be understood is whether there is one, two, or many types of time. The simplest view simply has the concept of time as an absolute. However, most organizations are not able to have every system, staff member, and customer online at the same time. Many operations are performed offline, on paper, or in a batch. At the very least, there is often the need to allow operations to be performed offline when the network has failed.

Such an approach means that there are two times associated with every event. The first is the event time (when it happened) and the second is the time when it is posted to the database of record (when it was recorded). The latter is the point of reconciliation.

Granularity is simply a way of determining what the most atomic level of detail that needs to be stored about any event such as a transaction. It can be a second, a millisecond, or even less. Each instance is then instantiated in a reference table.

The good news is that while the reference table would be long if it was actually created, there is no real need with automatic functions able to perform the function virtually.

Some modelers, at this point, would simply ask why the time and date functions within the database are not sufficient. The answer to this is that with a formal master data approach to time it is possible to enforce referential integrity and ensure that events are properly matched.

Further, time hierarchies can be created. Some examples of these hierarchies can include Hour → Day → Week → Year and Hour → Day → Month →Year. Such an approach ensures the correct encapsulation of reporting periods and similar concepts. Time, as with all master data, permits multiple hierarchies. Events can be associated at any level of a hierarchy.

GRANULARITY, TERMINOLOGY, AND HIERARCHIES

Time is not the only concept that needs a consistent approach to granularity and hierarchies. Almost every master data concept has some element of granularity and hierarchy. This is what makes integration across the enterprise so difficult.

For instance, people (such as clients) have many associations in which they are members, such as family groups, work colleagues, and locations. For different businesses, these can be relevant in some circumstances. Problems arise when different systems create, update, or delete at different levels of granularity.

In 1999, NASA lost an unmanned spacecraft on its approach to Mars after it hit the atmosphere rather than settling into a planned orbit. The investigation into the mishap found that the aerospace company that was responsible for the calculations used to fire the thrusters during the mission was sending information to NASA in Imperial units, using pounds to measure force rather than the metric equivalent of newtons.

Importantly, the investigation did not find that the subcontractor was at fault. While they should have been using the same metric units in communication with NASA, the committee found that there should have been better error checking and standardization processes in place to catch such inconsistencies.

Over time, every division within every organization will develop its own unique language for master data items such as products and locations. For instance, one division might call the head office *corporate* while another might call it *group*. Such differences appear on the surface to be superficial until there is a mistake that brings down the equivalent of NASA's Mars spaceship.

Whenever an enterprise approach to information management, and master data management in particular, is proposed there are those within the organization who are supportive as long as it doesn't stop them from working exactly the way they always have in the past. These stakeholders often know that computers are capable of supporting mapping tables when the two terms are translated.

The job of those responsible for the initiative is to argue fervently against an approach that permits the same item to be given two or more different names. While translations work, you only have to look at the United Nations to realize that they are less than perfect! Worse, the impact of master data extends much further than the reference data that it represents because master data links to other items of the same genre in a hierarchy (such as people within a family) as well as dimensioning the measures and metrics (effectively becoming the units of the enterprise). Master data even categorizes other master data (e.g., location can categorize customer and staff can categorize asset).

Keeping all of this in mind, there are three rules of master data that should be adhered to.

RULE 1: CONSISTENT TERMINOLOGY

The first rule is that master data should be described once for the whole enterprise. That includes both the field name and the content.

For instance, some divisions might refer to a *client* while others refer to a *customer*. While both words have very similar definitions, one implies the purchasing of complex services and the other implies a more transient relationship.

Within the client and customer field, one division might have a client called *ABC Corporation Inc.*, while another division might call them a customer with a name *ABC Corp.* Any visual review of the two names suggests they are the same company. However, attempts to integrate a client and a customer with different names are likely to fail.

RULE 2: EVERYONE OWNS THE HIERARCHIES

The second rule is that master data items belong to a hierarchy. Every publisher and subscriber to that master data must respect the hierarchy and do nothing that puts its integrity at risk.

For example, a bank might have an institutional division that provides credit facilities only to parent corporate entities while a business division might service individual companies within the group. The hierarchy might look something like this:

ABC Corporation Inc.
         ↳   Tyre Fitters Pty Ltd
         ↳   Widget Manufacturing Pty Ltd
                           ↳   Widget Retail Pty Ltd
         ↳   Milk Bars Pty Ltd

Although the institutional division has no interest in anything below ABC Corporation Inc., they need to be respectful of the child entities and their use by the business division. This can be significant during mergers and acquisitions when the institutional division could be the first to be notified and make updates to the master data.

RULE 3: CONSISTENT GRANULARITY

The third rule is that master data should operate at the same level of detail or granularity across the enterprise.

Many location-based databases have failed to give correct results because this rule has been broken. If the database is capable of storing a position down to a street address or a set of coordinates then some programmers take shortcuts and position events that occur over a wide area (such as a natural disaster in the case of an insurance system) exactly based on the center of the event.

For instance, a local government council might record the location of facilities using a table as shown in Table 12.1. In this case, there is both a park with a meaningful area and a fire hose that is likely to be at a specific point.

As with the hierarchy, this is solved by ensuring that events are described in terms of area and position or by creating a hierarchy that allows different processes

Table 12.1 Table of Facilities

Facility	Latitude	Longitude
Becketts Park	37°48′39.92″ S	145°05′28.84″ E
Becketts Park Fire Hose	37°48′39.92″ S	145°05′28.84″ E
...		

to use the appropriate level of granularity. In the case of the example, the park and the fire hose could be described in terms of area (with the area for the hose being trivial) or a hierarchy could be created that divides those facilities with the concept of area from those that exist at just a point.

RECONCILING INCONSISTENCIES

The one certainty of master data is that inconsistencies will arise. Even the most stable system with robust business rules for updates will find itself in the position where an errant process or network outage causes two inconsistent updates to be applied to the same logical record.

The most important thing is that any technology solution to master data does not permit overwrites; rather, all changes are tracked. It is also not sufficient to say that the most recent update is applied. If any change is going to have an impact on linkages or to analysis made using the data, there needs to be a mechanism to notify all stakeholders.

This can only be achieved if the Metadata model takes account of the application of the data at all four layers of the architecture.

SLOWLY CHANGING DIMENSIONS

In dimensional data warehousing (described as a *Kimball-style Data Warehouse*), the dimensions provide the user navigation. Periodically details of relationships, names, and other details can change. When this occurs, modelers face the important dilemma of whether to change history or to only apply the change going forward.

For instance, consider a supermarket that stocks long-life milk (the kind that doesn't require refrigeration until opened). The supermarket has a product hierarchy that groups according to the categories of fresh food, dairy, and packaged food. Long-life milk is initially associated with the dairy category:

Dairy

⤷ Long-life milk
⤷ Fresh milk

Fresh food
      ↳   Apples
Packaged food
      ↳   Baked beans

After a period of time, an executive decision is made to categorize long-life milk under packaged food rather than dairy. The new hierarchy looks like this:

Dairy
      ↳   Fresh milk
Fresh food
      ↳   Apples
Packaged food
      ↳   Baked beans
      ↳   Long-life milk

With one record of the master data, once this change is implemented, all four information layers are immediately updated. The problem occurs then in reporting and analysis. With the product dimension (which is simply the product master data) updated, any reporting of categories (dairy versus fresh food versus packaged food) is immediately changed both going forward and historically. That is, the results that were reported in 2007 cannot be duplicated, as dairy will be reduced (and packaged food increased) by the amount of long-life milk that was sold. If the change was made on August 1, 2008, then two reports might look something like Figure 12.3.

In this case, the amount of long-life milk sales in 2007 was $72,653.98. Dairy has been reduced by this amount and packaged food increased. In some cases, such a recasting of history is appropriate and in some other cases it doesn't matter. However, most of the time, it is a problem that needs to be carefully managed.

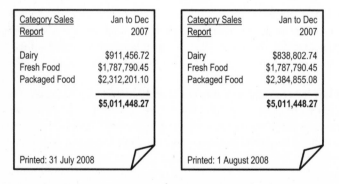

Category Sales Report	Jan to Dec 2007
Dairy	$911,456.72
Fresh Food	$1,787,790.45
Packaged Food	$2,312,201.10
	$5,011,448.27
Printed: 31 July 2008	

Category Sales Report	Jan to Dec 2007
Dairy	$838,802.74
Fresh Food	$1,787,790.45
Packaged Food	$2,384,855.08
	$5,011,448.27
Printed: 1 August 2008	

Figure 12.3   Same Report Printed 24 Hours Apart after Master Data Change

If a report is analyzing sales as they were in 2007, then it is appropriate to leave the product dimension in its original form. On the other hand, if a report is being prepared for 2008 and compared to the same results in 2007, it is necessary to recast.

Updates to master data, particularly hierarchies, should be treated in the same way as the recording of the time of event versus the time of posting. When a report is requested, it should be possible to specify one of three possibilities. The first option should be to cast the entire report in terms of the master data and hierarchies as they are now. The second option should be to describe any time series information (such as this year versus last year) in the terms they were described at the time. The third is to depict all results in terms of how they could have looked at a particular, specified, point in time.

The first situation is the most common. When a change is made to organization structures, it is usual that all reporting going forward recognizes the change and wants historical data aggregated in the same way.

The second situation is most often required when a people or product analysis is being undertaken in the context in which they were at the time of the transactions. For example, in the supermarket example, it may make sense to look at sales for 2007 in terms of long-life milk being part of the dairy category since that is also how they were managed.

Finally, it must always be possible, if only from an audit perspective, to be able to provide an approach to reproduce historical reports in the future that are an exact replica of those that were created in the past.

CUSTOMER DATA INTEGRATION

Customer data integration (CDI) is a specific form of master data management that brings together customer and client data across the enterprise. CDI has become very popular as a result of difficulties that businesses have experienced implementing customer relationship management systems.

A CDI solution is simply a master data management architecture that is dedicated to the customer dimension. Such an approach makes it much easier to implement customer relationship management systems successfully. However, it is important that CDI solutions deal with all four layers of information.

EXTENDING THE METADATA MODEL

Master data management is an increasingly popular approach to managing the complex information found in almost every organization. That popularity is due in part to a better understanding of the role of master data in acting as the dimensions that are used to navigate the business. At a more negative level, the enthusiasm for the approach is due to negative perceptions on the complexity of implementing enterprise decision support solutions.

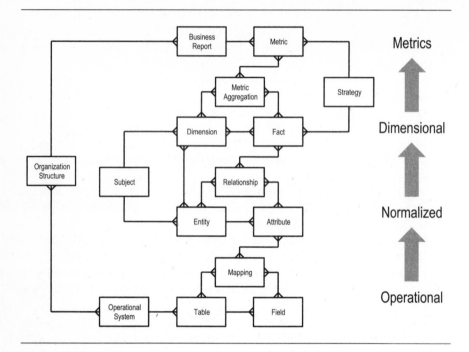

Figure 12.4 Example Metadata Model

As with any aspect of information management, it needs to be implemented in a systematic way without compromising the underlying principles. The best tool available is the Enterprise Metadata model described in Chapter 7 and extended in Chapter 11. It is useful to recall the example Metadata model used to describe the four layers of information found in every enterprise, shown again in Figure 12.4.

The model can now be extended to meet the requirements of slowly changing dimensions (SCD) as shown in Figure 12.5. Four new objects have been added: master data, persistent hierarchy, temporal hierarchy, and synchronization.

The *master data* object is simply a record of the master data attributes and map directly to the normalized model attribute object that describes all attributes and how they fit into the enterprise. The link to the normalized model provides the connection in to the dimension object.

The *persistent hierarchy* object describes the master hierarchies dealing with the situation in which a consistent view of all data across all time is required. The *temporal hierarchy* object describes the same hierarchies but takes into account changes over time so that a reconciliation can be made between different points in time.

Finally, the *synchronization* object links to the mapping between tables and fields at an operational level and supports the process to synchronize master data over multiple systems and across organizational boundaries.

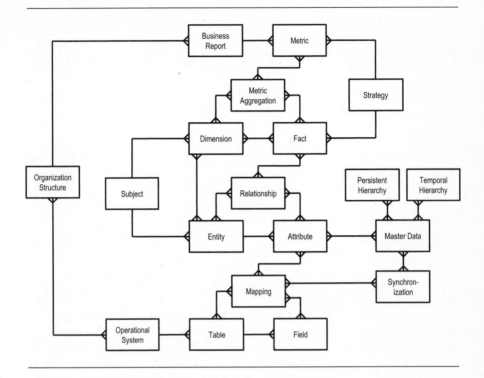

Figure 12.5   Metadata Model Extended to Include Master Data

TECHNOLOGY

Good technology is available to help organizations develop master data solutions but, like data warehousing, the answer must be found first within the enterprise. Every business needs to develop its own approach to master data management that is tailored to the way the four information layers are used and instantiated.

Good master data management is as much an organizational architecture and governance question as it is a technology issue. The technology team should take care to avoid providing stop-gap measures that appear to meet regulatory requirements as these seldom survive in the event of a real crisis—which is just the time when master data is the most critical.

If there is not a willingness to embrace the proper approaches as outlined in this chapter, it is advisable to focus first on the reconciliation rules and business issues that are already occurring due to differences between divisions. At least such an approach is likely to provide a management Band-Aid to solve the immediate problem while at the same time starting to educate the executive leadership about the deeper issues that the organization faces.

Chapter 13

Information and Data Quality

The quality of information is paramount. Ask business executives whether they have enough information to do their job and they will say no. Ask the same executives whether the information they do get is entirely trustworthy and they will also say no. Even more dramatic, consider the success and failure of major information technology initiatives. Systems that have been implemented with poor user interfaces but high-quality content are generally regarded as successful, whereas systems that have failed to correctly migrate data, even with the best user interfaces, are regarded as abject failures. In other words, in both business management and technology implementation, there is a direct causal relationship between the quality of information and successful outcomes.

While everyone agrees that data quality is important, there is very little that is truly agreed about either measuring or improving data quality. The problem seems to relate to a common misunderstanding about how to measure or manage the quality of information. Some of the techniques are sophisticated while others simply require a logical and consistent approach.

SPREADSHEETS

As you know, yesterday Fannie Mae filed a Form 8-K/A with the SEC amending our third quarter press release to correct computational errors in that release. There were honest mistakes made in a spreadsheet used in the implementation of a new accounting standard.

—Jayne Shontell, Fannie Mae Senior Vice President
for Investor Relations, 2003

Shontell's admission of an error of more than $1 billion due to a spreadsheet error is becoming increasingly typical, with research from academics such as Raymond Panko[1] showing that between 20 percent and 40 percent of all spreadsheets contain errors, with up to 90 percent of spreadsheets containing more than 150 rows containing errors. Panko goes on to estimate a cell error rate (CER) of 5.2 percent; that is, more than 1 in 20 cells in an average spreadsheet contain an error in content or formula.

Worse, spreadsheet errors build on themselves. There is a well-accepted approach to calculating the error rate as a proportion of the overall result, first provided by

Table 13.1 Effect of Combining Multiple Spreadsheets

Number of Spreadsheets	Error Rate
1	0.052
2	0.101296
3	0.148029
4	0.192331
5	0.23433

Irving Lorge and Herbert Solomon in 1955.[2] The impact of errors on a process (such as calculating the aggregated financial result) is:

$$1-(1-e)^n$$

Where e is the rate of error in an individual step and n is the number of steps. Using Panko's cell error rate of 0.052 (5.2 percent), the rate of error rapidly grows as spreadsheets are derived from other spreadsheets, as shown in Table 13.1.

The conclusion is not only that it is vitally important that critical spreadsheets are closely checked but also that when spreadsheets have multiple levels of derivation that each level clearly references all of the spreadsheets that it is directly and indirectly dependent on. The user of the spreadsheet can then make sensible decisions about the reliability of the data that they are using.

REFERENCING

In the academic world, no major paper would be published without referencing its sources. Far too much information exists in every organization that has no context or defined source. Every time a scrap spreadsheet is held on a network server, it adds to this complexity, particularly in the context of verb-and-noun style computing as described in Chapter 8.

Unreferenced information has to be regarded as unreliable. People only trust information that they access in spreadsheets or documents if the material comes from a source they regard as inherently reliable and if the content is sufficiently detailed to be self-documenting. Such material represents a diminishingly small percentage of documents that can be found on most corporate networks.

Worse than unused analysis are the organizational myths that develop and are perpetuated by poor-quality research and documentation that is used by generation after generation of employees. Businesses often make assumptions about the relationships among customer groups, products, and suppliers based on evolved myths. Because these myths have been repeated in documents over many years, they are accepted as undisputable facts.

The advent of professional desktop publishing through spreadsheets and word-processing programs has made the problem even worse. Many workers today grew up in an era before such technology was commonly available and, as a result, make the subconscious assumption that anything that is presented in a professional form is likely to be accurate.

Information and data quality initiatives usually start by focusing on the structured data repositories. In fact, this is exactly the wrong approach. The only way to increase the quality of information is to ensure strong stakeholder buy-in to improvement initiatives. Executives don't write and run structured query language (SQL) against databases, so they don't intuitively support initiatives to improve the quality of these tables.

The correct approach is to ensure that every analysis document and spreadsheet properly references where the content came from. If some of the content is narrative conjecture, then this needs to be clearly stated. If the content of a document depends on the accuracy of another piece of analysis, it needs to reference the original document. If a document uses statistical or financial results from another spreadsheet, it needs to reference that spreadsheet. This referencing should be done regardless of the form, such as a document or a spreadsheet that is used to record the information. If a document provides original analysis on a database extract or query, it should provide a unique link to the metadata holding that query in such a way that an independent analyst can replicate the result.

An approach used by some organizations is to standardize the color coding of spreadsheets. One color (such as blue) indicates that the number is sourced from a structured report or query, another (such as green) indicates that the number is sourced from another spreadsheet or document, a third color (such as red) indicates the number has been manually entered, and a final number (such as black) indicates it is derived from something within the open spreadsheet.

For this type of referencing policy to be successful, it needs strong leadership and an active education campaign. Most organizations have had situations when poor referencing and quality have led to incorrect decisions, embarrassment, and duplication of effort.

FIT FOR PURPOSE

When there are references in place for a substantial proportion of analysis documents and spreadsheets, users of information will begin to ask questions about the reliability of the underlying structured data. A database is generally built with a specific purpose in mind, regardless of whether it was primarily operational or analytical in nature. When this data is sourced, it is important to be able to indicate that the data is suitable to be used for the purpose that is planned.

A classic challenge is the *instance versus frequency* problem. One of the most common analytical mistakes that is made is to count events as unique members of a population. Consider the sale of tickets to football matches. A database that

Table 13.2 Football Attendance for April

Date	A-Reserve	B-Reserve	C-Reserve	Total
5-Apr-08	590	7,112	15,406	23,108
12-Apr-08	789	6,201	17,890	24,880
19-Apr-08	652	3,900	16,534	21,086
26-Apr-08	645	5,867	18,753	25,265
Total	**2,676**	**23,080**	**68,583**	**94,339**

shows how many tickets are sold by match might look something like Table 13.2 for April 2008.

Table 13.2 shows that 94,339 tickets were sold to football matches in April; however, this is often written as "94,339 patrons attended the football in April." In fact, from this information, there could be as few as 25,265 unique patrons (assuming the maximum duplication between the matches). Clearly the two extremes of interpretation would affect decisions about investing in membership drives.

The instance versus frequency problem is an example of the need for precise metadata and quality referencing within documents. The former would ensure that anyone looking at the meaning of the April numbers knows that they represent ticket sales not patron attendance while the latter ensures that use of the aggregate results can be tied-back to the original query and associated metadata.

A similar issue can be referred to as the *proximity versus confidence* problem, which is the level of confidence in associating imperfect data. The most common example is the management of customer data and the associations between customers. Consider Figure 13.1, which shows a common example of such associations and associated confidence.

On the *x*-axis are four groups: individual, close-family, extended-family, and marketing groups. Individuals represent the records that are assumed to belong to the same individual, close-family records associate spouses and other immediate family members (often treated as households). Extended family brings together concepts of wider relationships and finally the marketing groups are loose associations that are relevant (for instance, all the records associated with customers employed in the same workplace).

On the *y*-axis, the concept of uncertainty (the inverse of confidence) is expressed.

The first graduation is the legal association between records. A *legal* level of confidence means that you would be prepared to go to court using the identities built up through the associations. Commonly, this means that a service will be granted or denied based on these associations without further input from the individuals referenced.

The next level of confidence is identified as *marketing*, which indicates that the records associated with an individual or grouping is sufficient for the purpose of directly addressing the customers; however, it is believed that there is a material error rate in the data matching.

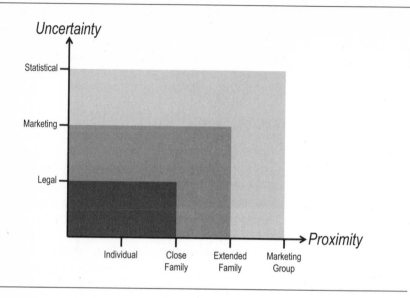

Figure 13.1 Graph of Proximity versus Uncertainty

Finally, there is the level of confidence associated with a statistical data set. Far more use should be made of statistical data than is currently the case. There can be association between multiple records that is statistically significant but which is not sufficiently strong to support individual contact. One purpose of this level of confidence is to initiate proactive cleanup and contact. Another is to support population analysis. When research is being done using the number of customers in a given demographic group, a decision has to be made about which data set is appropriate to be used. The number of individuals that are uniquely identified to a legal level of confidence is less than the number that are identified to a statistical level. The latter is the most accurate data set to use for a population analysis.

MEASURING STRUCTURED DATA QUALITY

There are three key measures that should be applied to the data residing in a database: *completeness*, *compliance*, and *accuracy*. The completeness measure provides a count of how many records in a data set are missing one or more details. The compliance measure counts the records that fail to meet business rules on each record. The accuracy measure estimates using statistical and other techniques whether there are likely to be errors in the data set.

The completeness measure is the easiest to calculate. For the data set being measured, identify the fields that should be completed because not every field may be necessary in every important business scenario (this requires judgment). At a later stage, a bias will be added. Table 13.3 applies this principle in a worked example of an asset database.

In this example, there are three rows and four fields that are identified as required. Of these fields, two have not been provided (Purchase Price in row one and Purchase Date in row two). Without taking any bias into account, the row completeness measure is:

$$\frac{complete}{required} = \frac{10}{12} = 83\%$$

The compliance measure requires a set of business rules to be applied to each of the fields. Each rule should provide constraints based on one or more fields within the data set.

We can now apply Table 13.4 to Table 13.3. Row 1 complies with all rules (it doesn't break rule 5 as the null in Purchase Price was identified under completeness). Row 2 breaks rule 2 (it doesn't break rule 1 as the null in Purchase Date was identified under completeness). Row 3 breaks rule 4 and rule 5. There are 5 rules and 3 rows with all but three passing. The compliance measure is:

$$\frac{passed\ rules}{rule\ instances} = \frac{12}{15} = 80\%$$

Completeness is the simplest test that can be applied to a data set; compliance requires more work to design the rules. Accuracy, however, requires substantial understanding of the data and detective work to design tests that determine whether

Table 13.3   Example Table

Field	Asset Name	Purchase Date	Location	Warranty Expires	Purchase Price
Required	Yes	Yes	Yes	No	Yes
Row 1	Table	23 Jan 2004	Room 12.3.43		
Row 2	Chair		Office 34.4.4	15 Mar 2006	$230.00
Row 3	Desk	20 Aug 2007	Office 19.7.2	20 Aug 2004	$1,110,000.00

Table 13.4   Example Rules

#	Field	Rule
1	Purchase Date	Must be valid date
2	Location	Must start with "Room" or "Office"
3	Warranty Expires	Must be null or a valid date
4	Warranty Expires	Warranty Expires must be greater than Purchase Date
5	Purchase Price	Must be between $0 and $100,000 (reasonable test)

it is correct. Accuracy tests determine whether a value that appears to be complete and complies with the ranges and other business rules is actually right.

There are two underlying methods that are used to determine accuracy. The first is *triangulation*, where other data is used as a point of reconciliation or comparison. The second is *statistical analysis,* which looks at the population and compares it to a known distribution.

The triangulation method uses other data sourced in different ways to reconcile or validate the content in the target data set. The hardest aspect of this approach to data quality is to ensure that the second database is to some extent independent of the first. Triangulation can be applied to individual records or to the set as a whole.

An example of applying the technique to the asset data set shown in Table 13.3 would be to compare to the balance sheet deriving a total value of assets and comparing it to the depreciated assets determined from the data in the table. Such an approach would show which records were wrong (unless there was a usable posting for each individual asset that was not derived from the same source) but would indicate the magnitude of the variance.

Another example of using the triangulation method would be to compare a customer database with a warranty database that overlaps the same customer details. Ideally, a robust master data approach will, of course, make this test redundant.

The statistical tests that can be applied to data sets are particularly powerful if they have been carefully chosen for the particular task. For instance, most countries have good data available about their population. Any sample of people can be compared to the general population of the same country (or even demographic in some cases) in areas such as birth dates and surname distribution. Further, the addresses can be validated against known addresses provided by postal services and equivalent providers.

The statistical test allows the analyst to compare the data set to the general population and see if there is a statistically significant deviation. It does not prove whether a particular record is right or wrong.

The first thing to understand is the concept of *statistically significant*. For the comparison of a subset of a population (such as the members of a customer database as a subset of the general population) this means understanding whether the distribution of Smith, Jones, and Brown is across the surname population.

The margin for error is generally calculated as:

$$z\sqrt{\frac{p(1-p)}{n}}$$

Where z is the statistical *z-value* corresponding to the confidence required in Table 13.5, p is the proportion of the general population meeting a particular criteria, and n is the size of the data set being tested.

To illustrate, based on census data from 1990, the top five surnames in the United States population are shown in Table 13.6. Imagine you have a database of 100,000 customers. What is the population of Smith, Johnson, Williams, Jones, and

Table 13.5   z-values as a Function of Confidence

Percentage Confidence	z-Value
50	0.67
60	0.84
70	1.04
80	1.28
90	1.64
95	1.96
98	2.33
99	2.58

Table 13.6   Top Five Surnames in the United States

Name	Frequency	80 Percent Margin for 100,000 Population
SMITH	1.006%	0.040%
JOHNSON	0.81%	0.036%
WILLIAMS	0.699%	0.034%
JONES	0.621%	0.032%
BROWN	0.621%	0.032%

Brown? Based on the margin for error, you would expect the population to match the top five names within a range of plus or minus the third column of Table 13.6.

To illustrate further, if the number of people with the surname Brown in the customer database was either less than 589 or greater than 653 it should be reported that there is an 80 percent probability that the database contains errors. These numbers were calculated from Table 13.6 by multiplying the frequency by the population ($100,000 * \frac{0.621}{100}$) and then first subtracting (for the bottom of the range) the margin and then adding it.

Such an analysis can be carried out for any data for which general population statistics are available. Good examples include surname, first name, and dates of birth.

The decision for which z-value to use depends on the nature of the data that is being tested. The choice of z-value defines the magnitude of mismatch between the distribution of results in the data being tested and the general population that is required in order to conclude that there is a significant deviation (i.e., a data quality issue).

As a general rule, 80 percent confidence that there is an error is an appropriate threshold for most data sets. However, if the data is particularly critical and any error is high risk, then a much lower threshold could be picked, perhaps even as low as a 50 percent probability of an error being in the data. Conversely, if the data tends to be very random and a significant number of errors are acceptable, then a much higher threshold could be picked, perhaps even as high as 99 percent.

As an aside, dates are worthwhile to examine and dates of birth in particular. An insurance company found that the value entered in the date of birth field by some operators was not accurate. At first glance, they met all of the rules and were not any of the default values. However, they were clustered in a statistically significant way. In the insurer's case, it was found that a number of customer service staff were entering their own date of birth due to embarrassment to ask for (or reluctance by customers to provide) the correct date.

While truly random dates would be difficult to spot, more often than not users creating incorrect values will tend to enter a specific date or a small number of dates.

A SCORECARD

Due to increasing levels of regulation, such as the Sarbanes-Oxley legislation (where the CEO and the CFO certify the accuracy of their company's financial statements), businesses are becoming increasingly aware of the importance of measuring the quality of information. Most organizations who have had to comply with these types of requirement have implemented at least a first information quality review, usually presented in the form of a scorecard.

It is critical to present the completeness, compliance, and accuracy measures to business owners of the data in a way that they can understand. Too much detail about the quality makes it difficult to interpret or manage the information. Too little detail makes the data quality metrics meaningless.

The classic mistake of oversimplification presents the quality of a data set (such as the customer database) in terms of a single percentage ("the customer data is 84.3 percent correct"). This doesn't tell the business user anything about the usability of either the 84.3 percent that is claimed to be correct or the extent of the problem with the remaining 15.7 percent.

A more meaningful way of describing the content is in terms of completeness, compliance, and accuracy. Such a statement of quality should look more like this:

> 6.8% of customers in the database are missing data that is deemed to be important, while 4.1% of customers break one or more validation rules. An estimated further 4.8% of customer details have a statistically significant probability of being incorrect in some material way.

METADATA QUALITY

All of the data quality checks in the world are irrelevant if the underlying metadata is wrong. Metadata tends to be the forgotten detail, particularly when the database is believed to be well understood by the user community.

The best approach to measuring and improving the metadata is by direct user scoring and input. As described in earlier chapters, metadata must be available to users and must seek their ongoing contribution to improving information definitions. This can only happen if every major application includes a direct link to the metadata definitions and describes relationships.

With an active metadata community, a rating system can be easily implemented (much like the ratings associated with products in online stores and postings in message boards). Lowly rated items can be flagged for analyst intervention, although ideally the community will do the updates themselves.

EXTENDED METADATA MODEL

The Metadata model that we've developed is now extended in Figure 13.2 to include the data quality rules as they are defined in this chapter.

The concept of a quality measure is associated with the foundation logical concept of an attribute. Quality measures are the aggregation of rules needed to describe the quality in the form of confidence.

Each attribute would have more than one quality measure that would include the underlying completeness, compliance, and accuracy measures as well as the interpretation in the form of:

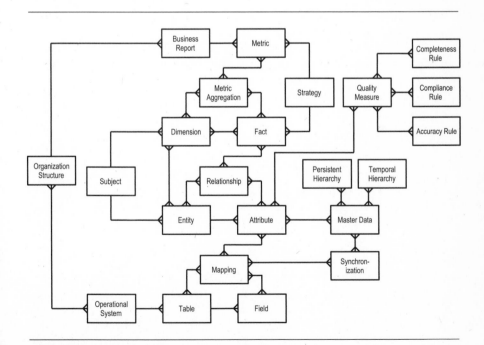

Figure 13.2 Metadata Model with Quality Measures

$x\%$ of records in the data set are missing data that is deemed to be important, while $y\%$ of records break one or more validation rules. An estimated further $z\%$ of records have a statistically significant probability of being incorrect in some material way.

NOTES

1. R. R. Panko (May 2008), "What We Know About Spreadsheet Errors." Available at http://panko.shidler.hawaii.edu/ssr/Mypapers/whatknow.htm.

2. I. Lorge and H. Solomon (1955), "Two Models of Group Behavior in the Solution of Eureka-Type Problems," *Psychometrika*, 20(2), 139–48.

Chapter 14

Security

Information is only able to be leveraged as an asset if it is made as broadly available as possible. There is a temptation to restrict access to all information assets on a need-to-know basis. In some ways, this appears to be the lowest-risk approach, but it can often have exactly the reverse effect as it leaves critical data that should be leveraged invisible to decision makers.

Invisible data has a way of appearing at the most inopportune time during a crisis (often in the hands of a journalist or litigant in court). Invisible data is also unlikely to be used in all aspects of internal decision making, which can lead to accusations of negligence.

Organizations do, however, have an obligation to tightly guard a large amount of information. For example, personal data associated with clients, employees, and other stakeholders should be secure. There is also a responsibility to look after proprietary methods, recipes, and other intellectual property when the organization is significantly ahead of the market.

While databases and operating systems offer security models, they should not be relied on without a good understanding of the principles on which they work, limitations, and the proprietary nature of their implementation. Almost all security works on either or both of two approaches.

The first approach is to restrict access to a given location or individual resource. For instance, the application may only be available to certain staff. The challenge that system designers have is to ensure that all access to the resources of the application are contained within the boundaries of the security model. Increasingly, systems are much more fluid about where they store information (refer back to Chapter 12 for the discussion on master data, for instance, which is often stored outside the core application). The worst situations is if underlying data is freely available to anyone who knows the network address, URL, or has the skill to use SQL to directly access the database.

The second approach is to encrypt the content while leaving access to the scrambled original material relatively open; the focus is on protecting the key through cryptography.

CRYPTOGRAPHY

Entire textbooks are written on the topic of cryptography, but at its core the concept is very simple. A message, referred to as the *clear text*, is converted into content

Table 14.1 Simple Substitution Cipher

Clear text	A	B	C	D	E	F	G	H	I	J	K	L	M
Offset key = 3	D	E	F	G	H	I	J	K	L	M	N	O	P

Clear text	N	O	P	Q	R	S	T	U	V	W	X	Y	Z
Offset key = 3	Q	R	S	T	U	V	W	X	Y	Z	A	B	C

using a cipher that is meaningless to anyone who doesn't have the key to the cipher to translate the content back to clear text. A *cipher* is simply an algorithm for a code, and the key is the variable that is applied to the cipher and is uniquely able to unscramble the text of the message.

Perhaps the simplest form of cipher is letter substitution in which each letter of the alphabet is replaced with another. In this form of cipher, the key might be the offset, so that a key value of 3 would mean that *A* is replaced by *D*, and *B* by *E* as shown in Table 14.1.

In this example, *HELLO* would be encoded as *KHOOR*. Only someone who knows the algorithm (cipher) and who has (or derives) the cipher key of 3 can convert *KHOOR* back to *HELLO*.

There is no reason why such a substitution approach needs to be the same for each letter. For instance, a key could be set such as {3, 5, 7}, which would mean that the first letter of the message would be offset by 3, the second by 5, the third by 7, and the fourth would start again at an offset of 3. *HELLO* would then become *LJVOT*.

Because code-breaking algorithms can draw on massive computing power, any pattern that is imbedded in the encrypted message puts the security of the cipher at risk. It is, contrary to public opinion, possible with today's technology and skills to encrypt something in such a way that it is not just practically secure but also that it is theoretically impregnable to all attacks regardless of what future technology becomes available.

In 2007, the British government had to admit to losing a computer disk in the mail containing the personal details of 25 million of its citizens. This type of mistake has become all too common as portable storage technologies have reached a capacity where they can hold the data associated with the entire population of any country. In fact, laptop computers now commonly have sufficient storage to theoretically store the personal details of every person on the planet. When this type of resource is misplaced, even if not maliciously, the risk is substantial and has to be made public to the embarrassment of the perpetrator.

If such materials really do need to be sent via physical means such as the mail, then they should not be left unencrypted and, in fact, the authority responsible should consider using an unbreakable code or at least something approaching it. The longer the key for a cipher, the harder the cipher is to break. In fact, if the key is the same length as the message text itself and it is truly random, then the message is entirely unbreakable without a copy of the key.

For instance, to absolutely securely encrypt, using the substitution cipher, the clear text *HELLO* then the key needs to be a set of five random numbers between 0 and 25. For instance {14, 1, 2, 0, 16}, converts *HELLO* to *VFNLE*. Because each number in the key set is independently random, even if someone knows that the first letter is *H* there is no way for them to determine what the rest of the letters in the encrypted message are.

Of course, that means that a copy of the key needs to be given to the receiving party. Imagine that the media being used is a CD or DVD. All that is needed is a partner CD or DVD completely filled with random numbers. Once generated, the key should be sent either before or after the data media. With the other half (either the data or key) only being sent once, confirmation is received that the other has been received safely and without tamper. Imagine how much public pain could have been avoided with such a simple step.

Forms of substitution cipher, with an appropriately large set, are often used to allow the data to be kept in a relatively public or less secure location while the key is more securely protected.

PUBLIC KEY CRYPTOGRAPHY

When information is to be made available to an individual, the providing system or person needs to supply them with the cipher key. The key is simply one or more numbers that can be transmitted in any one of a number of ways. It is not, however, appropriate to transmit a key over a computer network, as this then becomes the point of weakness. Even if a reasonable person would think it unlikely that anyone would be listening, it is poor administrative practice to leave such an opening.

The key needs to be provided securely. This can be done face-to-face or in the conventional mail. Increasingly, paired devices are being used that generate new keys in tandem. In all cases, however, the key distribution needs to be anticipated in advance and means the provision of real-time access is not possible.

A clever alternative was developed in the 1970s by several inventors concurrently, but the most famous and first publically described version was created by Ron Rivest, Adi Shamir, and Leonard Adleman and is known by their combined initials RSA. The alternative methods all take advantage of a so-called one-way function to one person to encrypt a message in such a way that only the intended recipient can reverse the encryption without any prior shared secret key. In *public key cryptography* the person who wants to receive confidential data makes a public key available that has a private key pair that they do not share. Anyone can have the public key but while it enables the encryption of the content, it is not sufficient to be able to unlock the message.

An illustrative example is shown in Figure 14.1. For Bob to send a message to Alice, he needs to use Alice's public key to encrypt the message. The public key can be made available to anyone (perhaps published on Alice's Web page) as it only allows for the encryption and not the decryption of the message.

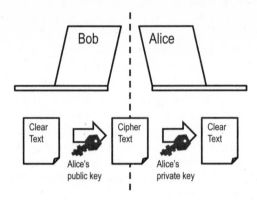

Figure 14.1   Bob and Alice Share a Message

The mathematics behind public key cryptography broadly depends on large number factorials. Although it is easy to multiply two large numbers together, there is no easy way to reverse the process and determine the factors of a large number.

Providing a variation of the product of these two numbers but keeping the numbers themselves secret allows, with the right cipher algorithm, such as RSA, Alice and Bob to share information without ever sharing a secret key.

It turns out that this form of process provides another benefit. Alice can encrypt a message using her private key that can be decrypted using her public key. The clever thing about this reverse process is that Alice can create a message that the world can read but only Alice could have created, that is, an electronic signature.

Public key cryptography in organizations is packaged as digital certificates that combine the key with the metadata describing the cipher. The most common standard for digital certificates is the International Telecommunication Union X.509 (ITU-T X.509) with public key infrastructure (PKI) becoming increasingly interoperable.

Today, most staff in most organizations have a digital certificate installed adhering to policies applied by enterprise security staff. Information management practitioners can, therefore, usually assume their existence and make use of PKI to manage the security of content.

APPLYING PKI

Digital certificates support signatures and encryption. They can be imbedded in office documents such as world-processor files, spreadsheets, presentations, and e-mails. The certificate validates that the author identified is legitimate (authenticity) and that the document has not been modified by anyone other than the author (integrity). Increasingly, attaching your certificate to a document is seen as a legal signature by regulatory authorities and courts (nonrepudiation). Digital certificates provide a protection against malicious misinformation being inserted into the enterprise, but they also help to make individuals accountable for all information that they are responsible for publishing.

Given the importance of cross-referencing information contained within documents to manage the quality of information (see Chapter 13), it is equally important to provide evidence that each reference is genuine. This becomes increasingly important when trusted references cross organizational boundaries; all e-mail should include the certificate of the sender.

E-mail, in particular, is a critical business tool that is vulnerable to spoofing where the *from* address is fraudulent. Many nontechnical users of e-mail are not aware how easy it is to send an e-mail that claims to come from someone else. Even e-mail distributed inside the walls of the enterprise and appearing to come from a company e-mail address could be sent from the outside the firewall. Adding a signature through a digital certificate to authenticate e-mails, and checking for the existence of these as a standard part of trusting messages, almost entirely removes this threat.

It is not just communication between two individuals that can benefit from secure identification; operational systems also need to provide evidence that activity was triggered by a known individual or system. For example, individual writes to database tables can also be signed in the same way, with a simple binary field provided for digital signature and a checksum of the fields in the row.

With the data properly identified, it can be encrypted using a simple cipher. Because public key cryptography requires that the public key of the recipient be used to encrypt content using this type of cipher, it doesn't make sense to store data in this encrypted form. To illustrate, imagine that Alice and Bob were both permitted to read a document or a row in a database. If the data were to be encrypted using public key cryptography, two copies would be required. The first copy would be encrypted using Alice's public key and the second using Bob's public key. Clearly this would be inefficient. There is another good reason for not using public key cryptography for encryption of stored information—the computing overhead is large. While appropriate for one-to-one messaging (e.g., encrypting the content of an e-mail) such an approach is inappropriate for the storage of information that is consumed by many people.

Instead, the most granular level of assigning access should be determined and simple substitution cipher created. Remember, as long as the key is secure, such a cipher is as secure as the key length, providing that the substitution is entirely random. If there are potentially three different groupings of document or database rows then as many keys are required for the relevant data sets. Avoid creating two groups that partially overlap each other because that requires the same data to be encrypted using two different keys.

The security administration module can now distribute the keys to individuals as they are granted access to the content. The distribution of the key is a one-to-one message and should be encrypted using public key cryptography using the recipient's public key. If the rights of an individual are revoked, then the key has to be regarded as compromised.

Encryption using these two methods (substitution ciphers and public key cryptography) is the method by which most database security is maintained. Most structured data solutions, however, only allow security groups to be set at the column level. This is less a technical constraint than reflecting the difficulty of supporting referential integrity and describing the complex rules completely generically.

Administrators of databases need to consider manually managing row-level security using tools within the database and dual ciphers as described in this chapter.

PREDICTING THE UNPREDICTABLE

Every day, somewhere in the world, there seems to be a newspaper article about a government agency, bank, or other service provider who fails to meet their public obligations because they didn't recognize that two events were related. The most public form of these unfortunately usually involve the exposure of children or other vulnerable citizens to avoidable risk.

There are two problems that usually lead to these tragedies. The first is the need to predict the unpredictable, the world is full of events that are obvious with hindsight but difficult to predict in advance. The second is maintaining the necessary balance between protecting the public and the individual rights of citizens.

This book has, if nothing else, put an emphasis on using information models and analysis to gain a deeper understanding of the business of the enterprise. Organizations are not defined by discrete metrics or key performance indicators. The organization is more than just a collection of business processes. Each algorithm sitting behind the collection of enterprise business rules feeds into the logical store of enterprise data.

A thorough understanding of the data of the business, and its underlying relational form, will provide deep insights into possible events and relationships that are potentially possible. It becomes practical to predict the events for which there is no precedent.

Just as important, such an approach allows for a meaningful matching between the experiences of other organizations and your own business. An abstract event that seems plausible is only meaningful when armed with an effective model it can be put in the context of how it could actually unfold.

PROTECTING AN INDIVIDUAL'S RIGHT TO PRIVACY

A very legitimate obligation is the protection of personal information. The tension that many, if not most, organizations feel is balancing this with the legitimate obligations and service that can be provided if the content is shared more widely. The obvious solution, from a marketing perspective, is often to encourage opt-in style marketing where individuals choose to allow their personal data to be shared more widely in the interests of receiving an enhanced service or the opportunity to receive offers that are of interest. Sometimes, though, the sharing relates to obligations, compliance, or law enforcement. In these cases, it is unlikely that the individuals being targeted would be willing to opt-in to a voluntary scheme, and good public policy should not require them to do so simply to avoid being seen as having something to hide.

The public key cryptography algorithms provide a mechanism to detect events that may require intervention without directly identifying the individual or even any details about each person. The technique requires that the original model is used to define trigger events; that is, the combination that taken together would indicate something that requires further investigation.

The principle behind the technique is that sensitive data falls into two categories. The first category is the content that is sensitive but is not required for the purposes of detecting a potential event. The second category is the data that is both sensitive and required to detect a potential event.

An illustrative example might be following an at-risk mother who potentially receives social services from multiple agencies. Her name and date of birth might be important for the purposes of identifying that the same person is involved in two related events in different agencies while her phone number is not required for the test.

For the sensitive data, it is a matter of creating a file that contains all of the data that is required to match between agencies but to obfuscate it in such a way that it can't be read by anyone other than the providing party. In principle, the process is relatively simple. The two agencies agree to a cipher such as a substitution cipher and generate a (different) key (which is not shared). The end result of the encryption process is that both keys are applied through the same cipher to the original file as shown in Figure 14.2. Note that if the cipher is sequence dependent (i.e., encrypting with two different keys in different sequences matters) then a third-party key needs to be applied by both Bob and Alice and then either Bob or Alice applies their key to both files simultaneously.

The end result is two encrypted files that cannot be read but that can be compared for matches in one or more fields. If *John Smith* is in both files, he will have been encrypted in the same way so that a match becomes possible (although *John Smith* may appear, for example, as *ojML jkllt*).

The major security issue in this approach to matching is that while the file is not in clear text, Bob and Alice both know what was in the file that they provided, thereby creating an opening to determine the key. While well-designed ciphers minimize this, it remains a risk if Bob and Alice do their own matching rather than pass it off to an independent third party.

In the event that the relationship between the organization and the third party, such as a customer, is a service-oriented and hopefully positive one, then there are a number of ways of maximizing the relationship data while respecting and

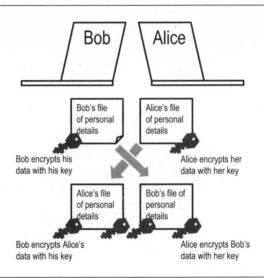

Figure 14.2   Cross-Encryption

enhancing the privacy of the individual. In Chapter 15, the concept of a *third-party data charter* will be introduced, which ensures that the relationship between the organization and the external party is described explicitly and positively to the benefit of both stakeholders.

A good relationship requires positive management by both parties, including mutual responsibility for personal and other private data. It is good practice to maintain a simple online register of what is permitted within the relationship and encouraging the customer or other individual to maintain the details of the relationship directly. Such an approach ensures that the maintenance of personal data is a shared responsibility with the benefit to the individual being that it is both up-to-date and that decisions about what communications are permitted are explicit online, including the rules around marketing and opting in or out of other forms of contact.

Transmission of personal details should be transparent and in some way communicated to the individual involved. Further, the content must always be thoroughly secured using the techniques described in this chapter. Where the material is leaving the safety of the enterprise network, encryption must be used even if it is being sent through courier or registered mail. If it is being transmitted over a public infrastructure such as the Internet, then it must also be encrypted particularly if the vehicle is an e-mail.

Increasingly such thorough management of personal data is not just good business practice it is government mandated. Preparing early can make a requirement into an opportunity to differentiate with stakeholders such as customers.

SECURING THE CONTENT VERSUS SECURING THE REFERENCE

The final comment on security in general and encryption in particular is that the information architecture needs to distinguish between security needs where the content needs to be protected versus situations where even the existence of the content needs to be protected.

This is particularly important in the light of verb-and-noun computing as described in Chapter 8. For instance, if the content relates to the financial results prior to publication then their existence is not a secret but their content must be heavily protected. On the other hand, the existence as well as the content of a set of files related to a planned takeover attempt on a rival company needs to be protected as even just knowing the existence of documents would be enough to tip off the market. Both of these objectives can be achieved by careful management of search indexes and encryption of keywords.

Chapter 15

Opening Up to the Crowd

It is tempting to consider your information as being your own and entirely under your own control. Of course, that isn't the case. Information from within the deepest vaults of the organization can be demanded by individuals (through various privacy rules), government regulators, courts, auditors, and any number of other potential stakeholders. Government agencies or departments often have the additional obligation to provide information based on various forms of Freedom of Information legislation and similar open government initiatives.

Every enterprise, regardless of its sector, needs a strategy to confidently know who should have access to every piece of information and to be comfortable that they understand what will be found now or in the future. Such a strategy needs to include information that goes beyond current access privileges and anticipates general requirements of the future. The history of privacy, freedom of information, and more targeted regulations, such as the Sarbanes-Oxley Laws, is that re-engineering systems to provide information on request after the event is an extremely expensive exercise.

Even in the absence of such requirements, having additional data early only increases the information available to decision makers, which is always a good thing. Organizations complying with the Sarbanes-Oxley rules have typically discovered weaknesses in their own processes as well as rich data sets associated with earlier activities that have been long forgotten.

For most organizations, it is not a matter of hiding information but rather avoiding situations that mean that there is anything to hide and ensuring that sensitive issues are visible to the leadership team early enough to take proactive action. At the time of a crisis, it isn't enough to just be able to confidently provide all the information, such as e-mail traffic related to a topic. If one of those e-mails implies that that there was an issue that was ignored then the business needs to have known about it much earlier. Not just early enough to have decided how best to deal with the crisis, but early enough to either correct the problem or (if the e-mail is poorly worded and doesn't deal with a real problem) make sure that issue is in context.

To illustrate the point, consider a maker of surgical equipment. New products are developed by teams of engineers and medical scientists who are brought together for the life of the project. Such environments tend to involve high pressure and large egos. From time to time, individuals overstep the mark and in trying to get their design point across write something in inflammatory e-mails to their project leaders. An example might be a hot-headed engineer developing surgical equipment who wants to change the design:

> This ... product has been poorly designed by Joe and is going to result in the death of patients!

Receiving such an e-mail, the responsible supervisor needs to look at the situation. If the supervisor finds that there is no risk and this is simply an issue of ego between two engineers, then he or she has good reason to counsel the author of the e-mail against making outrageous claims. Unfortunately, the e-mail stays on the record but the counseling is often likely to be verbal.

Consider what happens when five years later a patient sues the company for an injury related to the same piece of equipment. In this scenario, it doesn't matter that the issue raised by the e-mail is wrong; the tone it sets would be extremely damaging to the organization. Five years later, it is unlikely that the verbal conversations will be recalled; worse, the supervisor may no longer work for the company or may even have his or her own reasons for resenting the organization and take the opportunity to do damage. No business should leave themselves open to such risk.

A TAXONOMY FOR THE FUTURE

When external parties request information, they seldom limit themselves to a particular form (structured, unstructured, or semistructured records), which highlights the problems that the information management discipline faces with differing management approaches between structured and unstructured metadata (as discussed in Chapters 7 and 12).

It's up to the information management practitioner to design an approach which will identify the information elements against which a future search could be needed. At the very least, this should include the 15 items in the Dublin Core Metadata Element Set from the Dublin Core[1] initiative, as introduced in Chapter 7, plus an additional set shown in Table 15.1.

As a reminder, the 15 elements from Dublin Core are: Contributor, Coverage (scope), Creator, Date, Description, Format, (unique) Identifier, Language, Publisher, Relation (related object), Rights, Source, Subject, Title, and Type (nature or genre). The full description of the 15 data elements, and any future extensions, are maintained as part of the Dublin Core Web site at http://dublincore.org/documents/dces.

The Enterprise Metadata model can now be extended from previous chapters to include the concept of stakeholder attributes, as shown in Figure 15.1. The concept of *stakeholder attributes* links to the master data object in the bottom-right corner of the diagram.

Table 15.1   Additional Metadata Elements

Party	A generic term for an individual or organization. Any document or record could, for instance, relate to multiple staff, third-party organizations, and individual customers.
Project, Matter, or Issue	If work is done as discrete projects then the project should be identified consistently. In professional services, the term given is usually a *matter* and in areas dealing with problem management it is sometimes appropriate to refer to an *issue*.
Privilege	An indicator that the item may be subject to legal privilege such as some discussions involving lawyers or accountants. Note that the law on what can be treated as privileged varies across jurisdictions and over time, so the field should only be treated as an initial indication rather than as a primary filter.
Product or Asset	This term varies across sectors: for a manufacturer, it could be a tangible product line; for a resources company, it could be a mine or oil rig; for a telecommunications company, it might be a service offering.

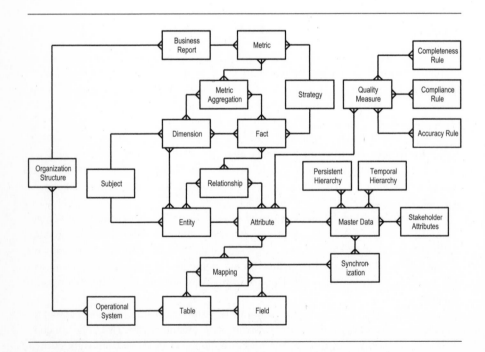

Figure 15.1   Metadata Model Extended to Include Stakeholder Attributes

POPULATING THE STAKEHOLDER ATTRIBUTES

The stakeholder attributes associated with application-generated structured data are relatively easy to govern as they should be controlled by systems with tight constraints. Most package software, including enterprise resource planning (ERP) systems, automatically track most if not all of the key items needed.

Careful planning is needed to populate the metadata associated with unstructured documents generated by office software such as e-mail, word processing, and spreadsheets. In each case, however, there needs to be a mechanism that is tightly governed to ensure the maintenance of the items.

For word-processing documents and spreadsheets, the fields should be mandatory and they should be saved to a registered location on the corporate network. While there are often good reasons for working offline (such as a laptop that is used when travelling), it should not be left to the individual to create the document and self-govern its later upload, rather a master document should be created in an enterprise content management (ECM) repository and an offline synchronization initiated between the laptop and the main repository. Major ECM vendors (such as FileNet, Microsoft SharePoint, and EMC Documentum) all support such functions in one way or another.

E-mail traffic is the major downfall of many organizations in crisis management. E-mail traffic has exploded due to its convenient and instant nature. Many workers report receiving hundreds of e-mails in their inboxes every day. With this quantity of e-mail, it is inevitable that some of it will get lost.

REDUCING E-MAIL TRAFFIC WITHIN PROJECTS

There are many good reasons for reducing e-mail traffic; however, regulatory and legal exposure has to be one of the most compelling. Consider again the earlier example of the surgical equipment manufacturer.

The exchange between the engineer and the supervisor was neither confidential nor sensitive. It was left on the record because it was of no immediate consequence. However, its impact years later could be catastrophic. Conversely, such an exchange could be significant and missed by a supervisor who lacks the experience of other engineers on the team. Either way, such a conversation should be conducted in an open online forum rather than through one-on-one e-mails.

The effect of posting such a comment on a discussion group that is open to all the members of the project team is usually to trigger immediate feedback from a number of people explaining why it is not a concern or suggesting further investigation. If the entire discussion is reexamined years later, the concern of the hot-headed (and perhaps terminated) engineer sits within a more sensible context.

In general, when discussion groups are created as voluntary forums within organizations to reduce e-mail, they tend to fail. Their failure is not a measure of the failure of the method, rather uncertainty on behalf of the poster about the reading of the material and whether it will enlist rapid and appropriate responses. An enterprise that, in response to risks such as those posed in this chapter, makes the use of discussion groups mandatory will find that without an e-mail alternative adoption will be by necessity will ensure that posts will be rapidly read and responses provided. Newer social media, such as Yammer (www.yammer.com), are helping make such discussions more straightforward.

E-mail within a project still needs to be allowed, but the author needs to be required to complete additional administrative steps to explain why the message relating to the project needs to be undertaken via e-mail. Further, there should be an e-mail address registered with a project folder that is copied on any correspondence.

MANAGING CUSTOMER E-MAIL

Customer relationship management (CRM) systems exist in most organizations, but the returns have often been inconsistent. Like many information management solutions, they rely on the effort of staff to record their interactions with customers without providing an immediate reward or benefit. This is another example where information currency (the payment for information) is usually not adequately considered.

To try to make CRM a more integral part of the staff's day-to-day operations, some CRM solutions are actually integrated with e-mail systems. The difficulty this creates is that the system inevitably become cumbersome since a significant amount, often the majority, of e-mail is not directly related to customer interactions. Just as important, the end result is usually not satisfactory, with the relationship still being owned by an individual staff member.

Most systems have interfaces that allow e-mail to be sent through the customer relationship, rather than directly from a staff member's e-mail account. This is done in a variety of ways and can be achieved by most e-mail administrators by setting up a simple set of parameters that can be added to the e-mail.

The replies are then received within the customer account and forwarded to the staff member. This means that while most e-mails can be dealt with by the original staff member, a team can work more closely together while still maintaining the personal relationship that the customer expects. More important, such a consolidation of customer communications allows the CRM to achieve its stated purpose of managing the whole relationship.

GENERAL E-MAIL

A staggering amount of e-mail is sent with only a few lines, suggesting that it is little more than a live conversation being carried out over e-mail. E-mail clients are not an efficient management tool for this type of communication and treats each as an independent document—subject to the same content management requirements as a formal report. Worse, the volume of e-mail that many staff is receiving is simply unsustainable and is a major drain on their time and enthusiasm.

It is good practice to move this type of discussion off the e-mail channel and onto instant messaging platforms. It is important to note that the rules on retention and access vary across jurisdictions; however, the critical point is that these platforms are designed to support rapid two-way conversations and encourage the inclusion of a third or further people to be done in a more useful way than relying on the assumption they read all of the earlier messages.

A lot of other e-mails are sent as part of informal document management, seeking comment on modifications that have been made to draft spreadsheets or word-processing files. Workflow and proper ECM solutions need to be put in place and should replace this type of e-mail conversation.

Broadcast e-mails should be replaced with online discussion, collaboration, and blogs from senior executives. Staff can be notified of important and time-sensitive communications using broadcast channels other than e-mail (for instance, a notice on every discussion group directing staff to the broadcast message). Roll-call-style logs should also be deployed to ensure everyone is reading the material that is intended for them.

With all of these changes in place, the volume of e-mail should be reduced from a flood to a trickle. The final culture change is to make it a matter of pride to receive less e-mail rather than encouraging staff to boast of how many are received.

PREPARING FOR THE UNKNOWN

If information, both structured and unstructured, is indexed in a form that anticipates future problems, the opportunity is created to forecast issues before they arise. An example of this kind of information is customers who appear to have unusual patterns of contact with the organization (perhaps a developing issue with their point of contact) or product teams that are generating massive amounts of draft documents that are generating heated discussion (as detected with text mining algorithms).

More complex fraud also becomes easier to detect. In financial services companies, for instance, it is useful to monitor unusual relationships between products and collateral groups. It is particularly interesting to know if customer collateral is being referenced across national boundaries suggesting an artificial spreading of risk.

One of the advantages of a comprehensive approach to information governance is that when there is an unusual request for data it can be easily centralized. As much as possible, templates should be anticipated for requests that could occur at short notice. Legal discovery, freedom of information, or privacy applications are some good examples of this type of requirement.

Such templates form part of the organization's information architecture and enable a rapid approach to assembling data in response to such requirements. In all cases, a quick response will save cost, reputation, and potentially avoid penalties or worse. At the very least, when dealing with complex litigation, freedom of information and the like, a manual search for information is costly. In many cases, the manual effort to track down information means that some items are missed. Supplying these later gives the impression either that something was being hidden or that the organization is incompetent. It is even worse when the omission is discovered first by the aggrieved party.

In other situations, there is an obligation to provide the information within a specified period of time. For instance, in the financial services sector many countries have introduced regulations to prevent money laundering. These rules put the onus on banks and other institutions to detect suspicious behavior based on the profile of cash activity. Even more demanding is the requirement by some countries that if a suspicious activity is detected, the institution has to assemble a case file of all documentation about the customer being investigated, including correspondence, in a tight timeframe.

THIRD-PARTY DATA CHARTERS

One of the advantages of a comprehensive approach to information handling is that all information about customers is integrated. It should make no difference whether they have a simple transactional relationship or play multiple party roles such as being a staff member, customer, and/or a director of the company and also a customer of that company. All the evidence indicates that people don't mind data being held about them and, in fact, want it to be actively used to provide a better service. For instance, consider the way customers interact with their bank. Before the 1990s, customers expected to have to tell their bank everything about themselves every time they dealt with a different branch. They often had to provide letters authorizing transactions to occur away from their home branch. Roll forward to today and we all expect every branch of our bank to know our account history. In fact, if they miss any detail or don't extrapolate items such as change of address, we get frustrated and consider moving our business elsewhere.

While consumers indicate they are concerned about the way their personal information is being held, business should not assume that this means that they don't want their details to be used. On the contrary, an organization that can determine what customer information is being used in what way can confidently develop a charter describing exactly how an individual's data will be used, for what purpose, and how they will benefit from that usage.

Such a charter can make promises such as "We will never . . ." and "We will always . . ." which is much stronger than the typical privacy commitments made to comply with various privacy regulations. Such charters are extremely powerful as they go beyond giving confidence to the consumer that their data won't be misused and actually give them a sense of the wider services that they offer— potentially helping to sell them on additional products. Businesses that are sufficiently sophisticated can go further and create opt-in services that go beyond marketing. They can offer to help a customer detect financial opportunities (in the case of investment services), better utility prices, or retail products that they are likely to be interested in.

Data should not be feared as a risk. Rather, it should be embraced as a strategic asset bringing business and customers into a closer symbiotic relationship.

INFORMATION IS DYNAMIC

Information is not static, nor is its status in the public's eye static. Some personal information or data about a company's product may be highly confidential until another stakeholder decides to take it public.

Blogging is a particular area of concern for many organizations with amateur journalists finding their own voice. Information in blog posts may belong entirely to the individual but involve a company and material that the company is otherwise holding privately on behalf of that individual. An example might be information about a business event (such as an insurance claim). Another might be the details of a product that was designed but never released.

The approach to developing a comprehensive information management strategy covering this type of information needs to be sophisticated. Staff needs to be counseled on their obligations to protect the privacy and confidentiality of company information when publishing in their personal blogs. Client contracts should, when appropriate, include confidentiality clauses that explicitly describe the ways information can be released. Public relations departments should be constantly monitoring all references to information that are likely to be relevant to the business including blogs and social network sites.

It is important to understand the strength and importance of the online social networking sites that allow users to maintain huge numbers of contacts outside of their business systems. Many business contacts invite staff to connect with them on these sites and while it would be useful to encourage the relationship to be recorded within business systems, it is inevitable that they will occur. Understanding the strength, breadth, and usage of these external networks is an important aspect of managing the complex information that is associated with the business.

POWER OF THE CROWD CAN IMPROVE YOUR DATA QUALITY

Despite the challenges that collaboration with staff and customers through social networks and other tools create by opening up the organization to more information flows, carefully planned strategies to leverage internal and external relationships can do much more than deliver high-quality Web sites for internal and external users. They can dramatically improve the fundamental quality of the organization's data.

When people think of data quality they often focus first on customer data. One of the best ways to ensure that customer data is right is to provide a way for customers to update their details online. On its own, this is an important capability, but to be really effective it needs to be linked to something that the customer regularly does on the Web, such as reviewing their accounts, orders, or other interactions with your organization. Truly effective businesses make updating customer details part of every interaction and available to all stakeholders in the data, effectively building a Facebook-like facility for their customers identifying relationships (friends), preferences, and activities.

Apart from enhanced customer service, it is worth remembering that it is much harder to maintain a fraudulent identify when you are connected through multiple relationships and you have to maintain an exponential number of fronts.

Business data includes much more than just customer details. Online collaboration both inside and outside the enterprise can enhance almost all data in some way. One of the most common problems businesses face is maintaining an accurate understanding of the definition of complex business terminology. Every organization develops its own language and expects staff, customers, and business partners to understand it. Worse, few maintain a dictionary of this language.

Consider creating a dictionary with components that are visible internally, other parts to business partners, and a relevant subset to the world in general. To really leverage the power of the Web, make this dictionary readily updatable (even using a wiki). While open to misuse, it is unlikely that internal staff or business partners who are easily traced will deliberately abuse the privilege. Online communities have shown that complex topics attract genuinely interested contributors who can often provide a better explanation to their peers that you could hope to publish either from an insight or simple labor perspective.

Finally, having learned to use collaboration to better maintain customer data and a data dictionary, it rapidly becomes obvious that many data sets would be candidates to be open to a wider community for monitoring, comment, or even enhancement. Examples might include lists of branches, community contacts, and products. In the last case, suppliers could make changes that flow through the supply chain with automated updates to customer catalogs.

The instinctive fear that many organizations feel about opening their content up for collaboration is often disproportionate to the real risk of misuse. Succumbing to this fear without careful consideration means they miss out on the power that the crowd can bring to almost every enterprise.

NOTE

1. The Dublin Core Metadata Initiative (DCMI). Available at http://dublincore.org.

Chapter 16

Building Incremental Knowledge

Marilyn vos Savant is a U.S. columnist and author who is well known for her column in *PARADE* magazine answering interesting, mostly mathematical, questions. Her most famous column in 1990 provided an answer to the "Monty Hall problem" (named after the well-known host of *Let's Make a Deal*). The letter positioned the reader as being a game-show contestant given the choice of three doors:

> Behind one door is a car; behind the others, goats. You pick a door, say No. 1, and the host, who knows what's behind the doors, opens another door, say No. 3, which has a goat. He then says to you, "Do you want to pick door No. 2?"

Should you change your choice of door? Before thinking about the answer to the question, it is important to add one point of clarification to the game-show question. The host knows which door the car is behind and to prolong the show's tension will always open a door with a goat behind it.

Marilyn vos Savant opened Pandora's box when she argued you should switch as you have a one-in-three chance with your first choice (door one), but a two-in-three chance if you change to door two. When this question and answer was published, it is reputed to have generated more controversy than almost any other topic in the magazine's history. Readers didn't just disagree with the answer; they were outraged! Before looking to why there was such a negative response to the answer, it is important to ensure that readers understand why vos Savant was right in the answer she gave. The best way of visualizing was also provided by vos Savant to gradually move the majority of readers to a correct understanding of the problem and solution.

Assume for the purpose of illustration that you are the contestant and that you pick door one. There are three possible locations for the car: doors one, two, or three. Since each time you are given the option of switching, there are six possible outcomes based on the three possible locations for the car together with whether you choose to switch or not. Remember, if the car is behind door two then the host will show you door three because he knows that the goat is there. Similarly, if the car is behind door three, then he will show you door two for the same reason. If the car is behind door one then he will show either door two or three randomly.

Table 16.1 All Six Scenarios When You've Picked Door One

	Door with Car	Host opens	Do you change?	Result
Scenario A	Door 1	Door 2 or 3	Yes	Lose
Scenario B	Door 1	Door 2 or 3	No	Win
Scenario C	Door 2	Door 3	Yes	Win
Scenario D	Door 2	Door 3	No	Lose
Scenario E	Door 3	Door 2	Yes	Win
Scenario F	Door 3	Door 2	No	Lose

The six possible scenarios are shown in Table 16.1.

In scenarios A, C, and E, you (as the contestant) switch and, in one case, lose (if the car was behind door one) but win if the car was behind either of doors two or three. In scenarios B, D, and F, you hold your ground and only win one out of three times. Marilyn vos Savant was right; switch and you double your chances of winning from one in three to two out of three.

If you are like most of the population, this result goes against your intuition. In fact, most people faced with the option of holding or changing stick with their initial decision. In effect, they've made an investment in that decision. This is another manifestation of the assumption that a single equation can define every problem and solution. Early-twentieth-century physicists have observed the elegance of the equations that seem to power the universe and held a view that discrete equations describe the rules of the universe. Modern physicists are beginning to realize that the rules that define everything around us are algorithmic rather than deterministic. That is, a set of steps have to be followed in order to solve a puzzle such as the orbit of a planet or the change in temperature of a gas.

Similarly, most people, in their initial analysis of information, look for one simple equation that will provide the unique answer. In the case of the game show, the intuitive equation was implied at the start of the question—"You're given a choice of three doors"—so the immediate equation that is derived by most readers for each door is:

$$probability(car) = \frac{1}{3}$$

With the new information provided, people may revise their estimate of probabilities based on the total information at the time, not the sequence in which it was provided. Given that only two doors remain, most people then estimate that the probability is the same on both doors:

$$revised\ probability(car) = \frac{1}{2}$$

A close examination of the problem shows, in the case of our game show, that the information changed or was enhanced by the game-show host after the first contestant choice and we need to recognize the change and the next step in processing the algorithm.

BAYESIAN PROBABILITIES

When new information is added into a problem, the revised probability of each outcome is sometimes called a *Bayesian probability,* after Thomas Bayes (1702–1761). Bayes was an English Nonconformist church minister and mathematician who was arguably one of a number of people to postulate that the probability of an event, *A*, occurring when additional information resulting from event *B* is provided, can be calculated by the following equation:

$$P(A|B) = \frac{P(B|A)P(A)}{P(B)}$$

Where $P(A|B)$ is the probability of *A* given *B*, $P(A)$ is the probability of event *A* occurring, $P(B)$ is the probability of event *B* and $P(B|A)$ is the probability of *B* given *A*.

In the case of our game show, we can define $P(A_1)$, $P(A_2)$, and $P(A_3)$ as the probability that the car is behind door 1, 2, or 3, respectively. Without any other information:

$$P(A_1) = P(A_2) = P(A_3) = \frac{1}{3}$$

As described in the problem statement, the host will only open the door hiding a goat not a car. In the scenario where door one is picked and the host opens door two revealing a goat, the probabilities of the car being behind the three doors are:

$$P(A_1|B) = \frac{P(B|A_1)P(A_1)}{P(B)} = \frac{\frac{1}{2} \cdot \frac{1}{3}}{\frac{1}{2}} = \frac{1}{3}$$

$P(B|A_1)$ is the probability that door two was opened by the host assuming that the car is behind door one

$$P(A_2|B) = \frac{P(B|A_2)P(A_2)}{P(B)} = \frac{0 \cdot \frac{1}{3}}{\frac{1}{2}} = 0$$

Given that the host opened door two showing a goat, there is no chance that the car is behind door two

$$P(A_3|B) = \frac{P(B|A_3)P(A_3)}{P(B)} = \frac{1 \cdot \frac{1}{3}}{\frac{1}{2}} = \frac{2}{3}$$

If the car is behind door three, then the host could only open door two, making $P(B|A_3) = 1$

Bayesian analysis allows us to accumulate knowledge and improve our analysis. In the field of statistics, Bayesian probabilities are not without controversy. Another school of thought is based around frequency statistics. This approach demands that all analysis be based on measured frequencies within either a population, a subset of a population, or an observational experiment.

While frequency statistics are a valid approach, and used heavily in the development of models, for analysts working with complex information and who have to deal with many probabilities that are often in multiple data sets, the techniques are often either impractical or completely impossible to apply.

The advantage of Bayesian probabilities over frequency statistics in information management is that probabilities are defined based upon the best knowledge at a point in time in a process that is then able to be refined algorithmically as the process develops. The knowledge can be incomplete and based on best estimates.

INFORMATION FROM PROCESSES

In Chapter 2 and discussed further in Chapter 6, Robert M. Losee's definition of *information* was introduced:

> Information is produced by all processes and it is the values of characteristics in the processes' output that are information.

The important aspect of this definition is its direct tie-in to processes. *Processes* are a form of algorithm executed over a period of time. Classic processes include supply chains, customer registration, and purchase transactions as well as staff and regulatory activities. Each process includes a set of steps, each of which generates information.

Consider the game show as a process in three steps. Step one, make an initial guess of door 1, 2, or 3. Step two, receive additional information in terms of a door being opened. Step three, make a revised guess based on the new information (leaving the choice the same or changing it). Step four, door is opened to reveal whether the guess was correct.

The information available at step four is very precise—the car is known to be behind door one, two, or three. Similarly, the information at step one is also precise, there is a one-in-three chance the car will be behind any particular door. That is the limit of the analysis in the information management approaches of many organizations that do not make information available for decision making during a process but only at either the beginning or the end of the process.

For fast-moving activities (such as completing a sale at a supermarket checkout) it might be acceptable to ignore business processes that are underway but this is inadequate for slower-moving processes, such as completing a home loan application or hiring new staff, which could last weeks or longer.

Alternatively, many other information management processes take a snapshot of information available at a particular point in time but take no account of the sequence in which information was added or how that can be leveraged. In the case of the game show, in step two the only information used in this approach is that one door has been opened by the host and hence there is a 50 percent probability that the car will be behind either one of the remaining doors. The Bayesian approach, on the other hand, recognizes that the sequence information provided is important for the interpretation; hence, the reason why $P(B|A)$ and $P(A|B)$ are on the opposite sides of the calculation.

One of the most famous applications of Bayesian probabilities is in the area of medical testing. If there is a disease that affects 0.1 percent of the population and a test is developed that has a 98 percent accuracy (that is a 2 percent false positive error rate) then intuition leads most observers (and unfortunately most medical practitioners in the real world) to assume that once tested positive there is a 98 percent chance that the patient is sick with the disease. In fact, such a test only provides 1 in 21 chances that the patient has the disease, or less than 5 percent.

The reason can be easily deduced using the Bayesian probability equation. For simplicity, assume the test provides no false negatives. Define event A to contracting the disease and B to be testing positive. In the general population:

$$P(A) = \frac{1}{1000}$$

For someone who has the disease, the probability of the test being positive is 1 given that the test does not cause any false negatives:

$$P(B|A) = 1$$

For the general population, the probability of testing positive is the probability of being sick with the disease (1 in 1000) plus the probability of a false positive (2 in 100):

$$P(B) = \frac{1}{1000} + \frac{2}{100} = \frac{21}{1000}$$

It is now easy to work out $P(A|B)$, that is the probability of being sick (A) if the 98 percent accurate test (B) comes back positive:

$$P(A|B) = \frac{P(B|A)P(A)}{P(B)} = \frac{1 \cdot \dfrac{1}{1000}}{\dfrac{21}{1000}} = \frac{1}{21}$$

That is, there is only 1 in 21 chances that a patient testing positive actually has the disease with a 98 percent accurate test. Not a good outcome for the poor patient who has been given the bad news and is probably not sick at all!

The medical test is a good example of a process. In step one, the patient asks the doctor about their chances of having the disease (event A); the best estimate the doctor can give is 1 in 1,000. In step two, the doctor refines the estimate by applying the test that comes back positive.

In a business sales environment, a typical process that might be considered is the sales pipeline. Measuring sales is very important to many companies who have to estimate their likely future revenue for public reporting and internal planning purposes. For complex products such as large machines or professional services, the sales process can run for many months so waiting until the end of the sales cycle means that the pipeline could be considerably underestimated. Not only is this bad for the balance sheet reporting, it also makes it difficult to do effective capacity planning.

Organizations run sales in a number of ways, but consider a simplified process that might have four steps. Step one establishes the customer contact. Step two qualifies their budget and establishes a new opportunity to win. Step three makes a proposal. Step four conducts the negotiation. In each of the four steps, event A should be defined as winning the contract and event B as the test applied.

In step one, the event B is the quality of the initial contact and the probability of winning assigned by the salesperson. This might occur as a result of a visit to a conference booth or a cold call. In any given sales cycle, an initial $P(A)$ can be established as the chances of selling to any target client in the general population of target clients. If there are 100 potential buyers of the service then the best estimate could be that there is 1 in 100 chance of selling to each of them in a given cycle so $P(A)$ is 0.01. $P(B)$ is the proportion of calls that provide a positive response to the sales discussion, at a booth it could be as high as 1 in 10. Evaluation of the probability is based on the quality of the contact, an arbitrary score provide by the staff member. $P(B|A)$ is the probability that a successful win will have been preceded by a positive sales contact, given that some clients like to play their cards close to their chest, this could be 1 in 2. The probability of winning a contract from a positive initial contact is therefore:

$$P(A|B) = \frac{P(B|A)P(A)}{P(B)} = \frac{\frac{1}{2} \cdot \frac{1}{100}}{\frac{1}{10}} = \frac{1}{20}$$

In step two, the event B is confirmation that the target client has budget and approval to buy the proposed product. With budget confirmed, it is often hard to know what the real relationship with the client is and sales staff are notorious for overestimating their chances of winning. The Bayesian probability technique gives a clear way of estimating using this increased piece of knowledge.

To estimate the new probability of winning based on the client confirming they have budget approval, $P(A|B)$ there needs to be an estimate from previous sales to similar clients of the probability of having a budget $P(B)$. For the purposes of this example, assume that 1 in 3 prospects have a budget. $P(A)$ is the estimated probability, absent to the new event B, carried forward from step one. $P(B|A)$, in this case, represents the probability of having budget given that the sale is won, which would be 1.0; that is, all won contracts would come from clients who have a budget. On this basis the estimated probability of winning the contract becomes:

$$P(A|B) = \frac{P(B|A)P(A)}{P(B)} = \frac{1 \cdot \frac{1}{20}}{\frac{1}{3}} = \frac{3}{20} = 0.15$$

Note that this is probably less than the sales staff might estimate at this point in the process. In this case, there may be additional information that should be treated as a new test, B as an intermediary step. This technique can often help to improve the business process itself.

In step three, a proposal is written and initial feedback is given by the client. Event B in this case is being successfully shortlisted. If there are five tenders and two are shortlisted, then $P(B)$ is 2 in 5. $P(A)$ is carried forward from step two (0.15). $P(B|A)$ represents the probability that winning a contract is preceded by being shortlisted (1.0); that is, all wins are preceded by being shortlisted. The revised estimate for winning after step three of the process becomes:

$$P(A|B) = \frac{P(B|A)P(A)}{P(B)} = \frac{1 \cdot \frac{3}{20}}{\frac{2}{5}} = \frac{15}{40} = 0.375$$

Finally there is the negotiation step. Obviously at this point there is more control in the process (it would be possible, for instance, to capitulate entirely to the client's position). All other factors being even, however, the probability of winning $P(A|B)$ is based on the previous estimated probability plus the probability of getting to the negotiating table. $P(A)$ is carried forward from step three and is 0.375. $P(B)$ is likely to be based on the number of participants in the shortlist; in this case 2. $P(B|A)$ is, once again, 1.0 as this represents the probability of being invited to negotiate given the fact that the contract is won. The revised probability that can be used as a baseline to decide negotiating tactics is:

$$P(A|B) = \frac{P(B|A)P(A)}{P(B)} = \frac{1 \cdot \frac{15}{40}}{\frac{1}{2}} = \frac{3}{4} = 0.75$$

All the way through the process, valuable information has been gained about the probability of winning that can be used to in a much more quantitative way than traditional point-in-time estimates by the sales team.

THE MIT BEER GAME

To demonstrate the complexity of business processes Jay Forrester and his team at the Massachusetts Institute of Technology (MIT) Sloan School of Management developed the Beer Distribution Game in the early 1960s. Based on his work on industrial dynamics, which in turn became the foundation for system dynamics, the game in its various versions is designed to demonstrate how even relatively simple business processes are sensitive to even minor variations in the information passed between the components or plays.

The simulation exercise provides a simple demonstration of perception versus reality inside a supply chain where information is deliberately constrained within each segment of the supply chain as shown in Figure 16.1.

None of the four players are allowed to share any of the information held by the others. Only the retailer knows (in most versions of the game) that the customer demand for beer remains static. Over time, massive supply variations occur and to the factory it looks like demand has become cyclical, often leading the factory and distributor to come up with complex models to predict the apparently variable supply.

In real life, this is sometimes interpreted in such a way as to create a sophisticated model for supply and demand that in turn leads to pricing fluctuations as different members of the supply chain try to manipulate demand to better manage their own costs and inventory. The beer game is a perfect illustration of the Bullwhip or Whiplash effect in distribution channels or chaos in action.

Players of the beer game find that they don't have sufficient information to discover this effect. In fact, the best way to understand what is really happening inside supply chain relationships is by simulating them using system dynamics and postulating different drivers for the flows as shown in Figure 16.2.

The Beer Game or Beer Distribution Game is available as a board game simulation or as an online Web-based tool from many different educational and system dynamics sources. It is a good way of demonstrating the complexity of the information that is generated by even relatively simple business processes. For information managers trying to convince their colleagues of the complexity of information, this can be used as an effective team-building exercise.

Perhaps most valuable, the insight that a Bayesian probability approach to testing different hypotheses about the demand cycle would indicate that the

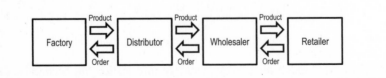

Figure 16.1   The MIT Beer Game

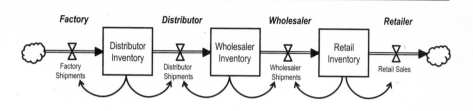

Figure 16.2   Simulation of the MIT Beer Game

input isn't simply cyclical. As a hint, start by setting event A as either the hypothesis that the demand is flat or that it is cyclical and then develop different tests, B.

HYPOTHESIS TESTING AND CONFIDENCE LEVELS

The Bayesian probability approach of using events A and B to test a hypothesis has a strong foundation in statistics.

Every analysis should contain two hypotheses. In statistics, the formal claim that is being made (such that the beer demand fluctuates) is called the *alternative hypothesis* and is designated by H_a. Why is the claim called an alternative? The burden of proof should be on the claim to prove it is correct whereas the null hypothesis, designated H_0, is the default assumed to be true unless the alternative is proven beyond reasonable statistical doubt.

Because formal hypothesis testing is done with two hypotheses, confidence should be built up in stages. Further, the probabilities used should develop on each other as described using Bayesian principles. In the example of the beer game, the data being analyzed by the factory should not go so far as to test that demand follows a particular trend; rather, it should first establish that there is any statistically significant fluctuation at all.

One testing approach that could be used in the Beer Game, to a reasonable degree of confidence that the demand varies (that is a high probability of event A), is to build a parallel simulation in which demand is constant (the null hypothesis) and to compare the demand from the distributor to real world demand of the game itself. For example, say in the real world, the mean demand is 24 cases per day and the simulation is tweaked to provide the same then a comparison can be made between each member of the two sets and the average or mean demand (in this case 24). The comparison is the standard deviation, s, and is calculated by:

$$s = \sqrt{\frac{\Sigma(x - \bar{x})^2}{n-1}}$$

Table 16.2 z-values as a Function of Confidence

Percentage Confidence	z-value
50	0.67
60	0.84
70	1.04
80	1.28
90	1.64
95	1.96
98	2.33
99	2.58

Where $\bar{x}$ is the mean of the data set (in this case 24). If the standard deviation of the real-world data is 23 and the standard deviation of the simulation is 15 over 100 cycles, then this can be interpreted by calculating the p-value which is the probability (between 0 and 1) that the null hypothesis is correct, hence to accept the alternative we generally want a p-value that is below .05.

Recall that a result derived from a data set can be measured using z-values as shown in Table 16.2. A 95 percent confidence correlation requires a z-value of 1.96. Recall also that the margin for error, which is the p-value in our hypothesis test, is calculated:

$$z\sqrt{\frac{p(1-p)}{n}}$$

For this statistical test, with a 95 percent confidence, assume p to be the proportion of the population that is inside 1 standard deviation (for our test we will use 56 or a proportion of 0.56) meaning that we are 95 percent sure that the standard deviation of the real world, if the null hypothesis is true unless the proportion of the population is outside the range of .56 plus or minus 0.1:

$$\pm 1.96\sqrt{\frac{.56(1-.56)}{100}} = \pm 0.10$$

If the real-world proportion that was within the given range is less than 46 percent or greater than 66 percent there is a strong case that the distribution is not consistent.

Any test applied in this way can be given confidence levels based on this population confidence formula:

$$z\sqrt{\frac{p(1-p)}{n}}$$

Simply set z to the value from Table 16.2 that corresponds to the confidence desired for the error bars (95 percent is a common choice, resulting in z being set to 1.96). The proportion of the population that meets the criteria being tested is assigned to the variable p. Finally, the number of elements in the population is assigned to the variable n.

Of course, there are a number of statistical tests to establish the covariance of two variables (the real world versus the simulation in this case), but whichever approach is used it needs to be fully described and a confidence level applied to it in this way.

In the earlier analysis of the sales process, the probability of each stage could have been further refined with error calculations. This would have been particularly valuable if a conservative balance sheet position was required. For instance, in the case of step two, the calculation included an estimate that 1 in 3 prospective clients were able to find the budget. This estimate was made by examining the sales database.

If the database contained 120 previous sales pursuits and 40 of them turned out to have found the budget, then the 1 in 3 estimate used for $P(B)$ was correct based on the population. Statistically, however, an error should be estimated. The proportion (p) should be set to 0.33. The z-value should be set to 1.96 and the population (n) set to 120. The new estimate for $P(B)$ should be:

$$P(B) = 0.33 \pm z\sqrt{\frac{p(1-p)}{n}} = 0.33 \pm 0.08$$

In turn, this provides a modified $P(A|B)$ that should include the confidence level:

$$P(A|B) = \frac{P(B|A)P(A)}{P(B)} = \frac{1 \cdot \frac{1}{20}}{\frac{1}{3} \pm 0.08} = 0.15 \pm 0.05$$

BUSINESS ACTIVITY MONITORING

Business activity monitoring (BAM) is a term first used by technology research firm Gartner to describe "real-time access to critical business performance indicators to improve the speed and effectiveness of business operations."[1] Since its definition, the term has gained wide acceptance as organizations have realized they need access to information during a business process rather than waiting until their conclusion.

BAM effectively allows leaders to move beyond individual metrics as an aggregation and to define algorithms that can be used to differentiate a business. Such an approach allows for a much greater degree of control over customer churn, approvals, risk management, assets, and other dynamic aspects of the business. For instance, consider again the four-step sales process defined in this chapter. A traditional business metric rewards sales staff based on the final outcome, which is the total amount of money spent with the business. A sales-based reward, bonus, or commission provides a direct linkage between the business result and the performance of the individual sales staff member.

The problem is that the winning of contracts tends to be binary; that is, it is either won or it is lost. If the business has a high volume of sales, then wins and losses will average out and hard-working sales executives will consistently earn their rewards. In businesses with a smaller number of high-value transactions, there is a great risk that a high-quality individual will do all the right things to be successful and will simply not be lucky enough to get a job over the line. Sometimes this is fine; it creates a hunger in the sales executive's mind to get future sales. However, often this results in manual intervention by the leadership team.

Rather than rely on such manual interventions, which may be seen by others as altering the rules during the game, it is possible to use BAM to identify measures within the process that benefit most from sales executive focus and reward those at a more granular level. Such an approach encourages fact-based decision making (as promoted within the governance frameworks of Chapter 3). Sales teams are thus encouraged to work the process to achieve the highest possible probability of winning while still chasing after the big jobs with the largest payback to the company as a whole.

BAM also allows sales management to supervise the overall pipeline and identify those leads that could benefit from greater focus or an alternative approach. Given knowledge of average behavior at each individual step and test (B) that is applied, BAM allows the organization to implement continual reporting on the performance of each pursuit. For instance, if the budget test for an individual opportunity indicates that there is ample capacity to purchase, but the previous relationship was not as strong as the mean across the cohort, then a substantial investment in relationship marketing might be justified.

With increasing focus on business controls, it is worth noting that such control points are naturally rich in data based on reconciliations, authorities, and external reviews. Any review of information opportunities could do worse than start by examining control points within documented processes and consider whether BAM could extend the usage and hence value of the information generated.

NOTE

1. D. McCoy (April 2002), "Business Activity Monitoring: Calm before the Storm," Gartner Inc. Available at www.gartner.com/resources/105500/105562/105562.pdf.

Chapter 17

Enterprise Information Architecture

The first generation of computing was focused on back-end batch processing intensive functions, such as managing bank account balances, calculating telephone bills, and producing financial statements. The amount of information involved in each of these functions was limited to the boundaries of the specific activity being undertaken.

The design for these types of systems was heavily focused on the calculation process. In this era of development, design documents included large system flow-charts defining the program steps that needed to be undertaken. The data resulting from each step was of little more consequence than managing its storage and retrieval.

The next generation of computer systems provided interactive functions for a wider range of staff, including those interacting with customers. Such computing solutions needed to be more intuitive, given the wider range of functions individuals were being asked to undertake, the reduced level of training resources that could be dedicated to this wider audience, and the inclusion of a large group of users who had little or no computing experience.

The first generation of the World Wide Web on the Internet spawned a much wider need to understand how information is consumed and encouraged designers of Web pages to design their sites very carefully, so the sites would meet the needs of all of their user community. This created the first generation of information architectures.

The term *information architecture* appears to have been first used by Richard S. Wurman during the 1976 AIA National Convention, Architecture of Information. Writing later on the topic, Wurman defines *information architecture* as "The ability to make the complex clear, and an emphasis on understanding as opposed to styling."[1] An alternative term for *information architecture* is *information design*, which implies that the layout is concerned with aesthetics rather than function. In business, and often in leisure activities, people will gravitate toward computer systems that give them the information they want even at the cost of aesthetics.

WEB SITE INFORMATION ARCHITECTURE

Web designers have taken the term *information architecture* and, for a period, they made it their own. The general consensus is that in this context, the information architecture documents the information contained on the Web site and all of the different ways that users will seek to navigate, link, and apply that information.

The definitive book on this subject is credited to Peter Morville and Louis Rosenfeld, titled *Information Architecture for the World Wide Web*[2] where they define *information architecture* in four parts:

1. The combination of organization, labeling, and navigation schemes within an information system.

2. The structural design of an information space to facilitate task completion and intuitive access to content.

3. The art and science of structuring and classifying Web sites and intranets to help people find and manage information.

4. An emerging discipline and community of practice focused on bringing principles of design and architecture to the digital landscape.

There are many ways of achieving a good information architecture in support of Web site design, but the principles that tend to be common include a clear linkage between the business goals and the information required to achieve them as well as a flexible approach to navigating to the same information based on the mind-set of the user.

Increasingly, good information architecture for Web site design involves structuring the metadata tags associated with individual pages in such a way that users of the site can find material easily using internal and external search engines. Tightly managing the page metadata involves having a good understanding of the search-based computing model described in Chapter 8.

EXTENDING THE INFORMATION ARCHITECTURE

The objectives of making Web sites easy to navigate, and to intuitively find information, is consistent with the objectives of information management to put information at the forefront of business thinking. The techniques of enterprise information management form the basis, when applied to an individual organization or business domain, of an information architecture.

The information architecture of an enterprise can never be static. It is rare indeed that the systems and information of a whole business are re-engineered from top to bottom in one program of work. The information architecture should be initiated for a specific goal associated with making better use of the information asset and then become a living part of the business strategy, usually under the stewardship

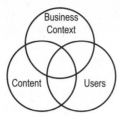

Figure 17.1   Domains of Information Architecture

of a chief data officer (CDO, as owner of the information asset) in partnership with the chief information officer (CIO, as owner of the technology assets).

The three domains of a good Information Architecture are fundamental to any business problem and are commonly drawn as shown in Figure 17.1.

BUSINESS CONTEXT

Business context provides the foundation for any set of solutions. The objectives and business processes that drive the business should be found within the business context. The development of an information architecture business context should draw heavily on the information governance analysis described in Chapter 3 and the overall business strategy of the executive team.

Recall that the Content model, as expressed in the four layers of information (see Chapter 11), ties the top layer (metrics) to the organizational strategy but the normalized (third) layer represents the fundamental objectives of the business. These objectives should be described in generic terms, leveraging the understanding of the normalized model as it develops.

USERS

The analysis of users of information needs to be described in terms of the information governance strategy and the identification of different user groups who are stakeholders in the information. Typically, this means understanding the usage of information at all levels of the organization and in each line of business. Such an analysis is not complete if it doesn't start at the board or equivalent governance level (such as the responsible government minister in a public sector department, or board of management in a nonprofit agency). At this level, information is consumed to ensure compliance with governance obligations and a better understanding of the recommendations being made as part of board submissions by executive management.

The executive team, who often join an organization with a limited tenure and a specific set of ambitious goals, need complex information directly tied to their strategy as they understand it on any given day. The information architecture must define the information the executive requires to fulfill the operational aspects of their role together with anticipation for the type of analysis the executive team is likely to want based on their strategic goals.

Middle managers have typically built up a picture of the information they use in their individual roles and have filled the gaps using complex spreadsheets. The information architecture should broadly describe the pattern of their information consumption and how they meet that need.

At the frontline, the operations of the business generate and consume information in every aspect of their responsibilities including manufacture of product, fulfillment of orders, and completion of customer transactions. Most organizations have invested in process flows, value diagrams, or product descriptions that can be leveraged to describe which data sets are developed where and when.

CONTENT

The content model should draw heavily on the four layers of information combined with the organizational structure and evolving Metadata model. The objective of the content section of the information architecture should be to introduce the detailed Metadata model as it evolves as well as unreconciled deviations to that model that exist in the systems that are already in place.

The Content model should be described in a way all stakeholders can use immediately. Designers of new Web pages should be linking in to the Content/Metadata model so that enterprise search applications meet the objectives of the Chapter 8 computing model. The data modelers developing data warehouses and other decision support systems need to be able to use the Metadata model to inform their choices at a physical data modeling level. The developers of spreadsheets (including end-users) should be able to meet the minimum information requirements, at least for referencing, required by the Metadata model. The procurers and developers of operational systems should be able to leverage the minimum standards required for information and its sharing between systems.

TOP-DOWN/BOTTOM-UP

The top-down elements of the enterprise information architecture should start with the four layers of information as described in Chapter 11. From there it should identify the master data (see Chapter 12) and the strategy for its management, the Information Governance model (from Chapter 3). An Enterprise Metadata model is needed to provide a structure for the enterprise information architecture and should become the foundation for the top two layers of information (metrics and dimensional views).

The bottom-up elements of the enterprise information architecture are far more detailed and time consuming. They should be completed in the context of each individual development project. The bottom up analysis should undertake an inventory of the information on hand and make estimates of the information entropy of each set, whether it is structured or unstructured and estimate the information entropy of the data set. If the individual store is in a structured form, the Small Worlds business measures should be calculated.

The flows of master data need to be documented between the different data set and points of control identified.

PRESENTATION FORMAT

There are as many ways of presenting an enterprise information architecture (EIA) as there are organizations, and each should be tailored to the culture and audience. Some organizations prefer big graphical representations on large sheets of paper pinned to the wall. Others do better if they are given an online view that can be dynamically updated. Ideally, an online approach is directly linked to the metadata so that it is self-perpetuating.

Table 17.1 is a starting approach for an online EIA. Because the EIA is a living document, it is usually advisable to develop it as an online set of Web pages.

PROJECT RESOURCING

The best EIA in the world, even when combined with the richest data, will not deliver results without a capable and motivated team. Ideally, the establishment of an EIA will be treated as a project placed near the top of the list of enterprise priorities. However, it is common to have made compromises to get to here. If that is the case, having to make compromises when it comes to the team is often mandated by the wider organization that needs to apply the best resources to other critical resources. Be careful. Keeping a project alive for another day by accepting team members who are second-rate, not wanted by other projects, or who do not have the core skills will result in a second-rate system that is worse than no system at all. Worse, the owner of the project will personally carry the stigma of the second-rate solution that is developed.

Occasionally political imperatives will demand that a person be appointed to a role for which they do not dedicate sufficient time or have sufficient skill. While this situation is to be avoided whenever possible, there are methods for managing the situation. A common example is an executive who wants to be the sponsor, but does not see the need to be active in that role. In which case, ensure there is a real shadow for that person who is the true sponsor and who has direct contact at sufficiently senior levels. It is important to find a way for this individual to be a hero

Table 17.1   Potential Contents for an Information Architecture

Introduction	Outline the objectives of the EIA and provide a narrative history of the project. Ideally emphasize strong executive sponsorship and tell a story about a problem encountered by the organization as a result of poor data or data usage in the past. From the introduction, provide links to each of the pages in the EIA.
Business Context, Users, and Content Domains	Provide a description of each of the three domains and provide the details described in this chapter.
Information Layers	Outline the meaning of the four layers of information (using extracts from Chapter 11 if that helps) and then put it in the context of the organization using worked examples. Provide links to the system inventory indexed by the four layers.
Enterprise Metadata	This page should contain the Metadata model and link directly to (or ideally be part of) the metadata repository user interface. A number of the sections of the EIA should include content directly generated from the metadata repository, the links should be clearly documented in this section.
Systems Inventory	This section should be automatically generated from a metadata table. There should be a list of systems that contain data, indexed by the four layers. The system inventory within the EIA should show which systems publish data (cross-reference to key data sets) and which subscribe to data. For those that provide data to users, there should be a cross-reference to the information users.
Master Data	This page should also be populated from the metadata repository, containing a list of master data items and cross-referencing to systems that create, read, update, or delete entries. Identify issues with consistent naming and hierarchies and identify a path to resolution with ownership at a business executive level.
Information Governance	Describe the information governance structure. Populate the individual contacts directly from the metadata repository so that they are maintained live.
Key Data Sets	Most organizations have a subset of data that is critical. Identify these data sets and cross-index to the systems inventory.
Data Set Metrics	Score each of the key data sets based on Small Worlds, Information Entropy, and Decision Entropy.
Information Flows	Show how information moves around the organization.
Information Users	Group the users in a meaningful way (by level, division, product, or perhaps culture) and cross-reference to the data sets they use and their preferred method of accessing the content.
Priority Standards	Don't overreach. Pick a few key data sets and define standard approaches to the data.
Priority Investments	Describe where the greatest benefits come from in terms of investment in system improvement, staff training, new analytical technology (such as a data warehouse), or better governance.
Data Quality Measures	This section should be generated automatically from the metadata repository and ideally populated in a dashboard view.

by linking their enthusiasm to a current issue or even crisis. Make sure that the issues get prioritized at the most senior levels of the organization and then seek their help to get a sponsor who is also at that executive team level.

INFORMATION TO SUPPORT DECISION MAKING

The EIA provides the foundation that enables every stakeholder to access the information they need, when they need it, and where they need it. Typically this information is used to support decisions. Some of those decisions are trivial, such as deciding which of two similar-looking names corresponds to the customer on the phone. Some of those decisions are complex, such as deciding whether to make a substantial capital investment.

CIOs have typically struggled to get the wider organization interested in questions of architecture, information strategy, or even information management. The EIA should be treated quite differently. Rather than being a tool to better manage technology (or its implementation) the EIA is the blueprint that can enable the whole business to get the information it needs when it needs it regardless of whether that need was previously anticipated. The EIA enables the information-driven business!

In the beginning, information-based decision support systems made an implicit promise: decision-making support for everybody, every day, in every aspect of their lives. After all, most decisions that people make, whether at work or play, have a large logical element that could benefit from bringing together all the facts.

Have these decision support systems lived up to its promise? Most business users would admit that to an extent they have met a critical need, but the implied promise went a lot further than today's solutions are able to go. To truly achieve the goal, information in support of decision making needs to be as ubiquitous as many other technologies have, or will, become. The key is market penetration, getting the right information onto everyone's desktop and getting an investment in terms of their time; that is, using the information available to them to make fact-based decisions.

To position the EIA with the entire organization, it is worth thinking for a moment about the barriers to using information-based decision support systems.

The first barrier is availability. Is the decision-making facility available at the time the decision needs to be made? Most people are so overloaded that they are forced work on the just-in-time principle.

The second barrier is complexity. Where many information technology products try to automate and simplify existing processes, decision support does quite the opposite. Decision support is about achieving a better outcome for the same, or a little more, work. If it looks hard, people will find excuses to avoid using it.

The third barrier is cost. Cost should always be considered a barrier. If the price of decision support products, implementation, or training is too high, then these products won't get used.

The MicroStrategy President and CEO, Michael Saylor, refers to the concept of getting information to everyone as *Query Tone*. Saylor argues that a query capability should be as pervasive as the dial-tone on a telephone. In his view, the dial tone represents the ability to pick up a phone and speak to anyone in the world while Query Tone represents the ability to turn on a computer and ask any question of any database anywhere in the world. Having said that, while the telephone dial tone might mean that it is possible to talk to anyone in the world, it often seems to mean that while people have more contacts than ever before, they spend less time talking to their friends and family. Unfortunately, having a technological capability doesn't necessarily mean that it gets used for the best purposes.

With an EIA, a road map can be drawn so information-based decision supporting can be used by every part of the organization to assist every decision-making process by the seamless integration with decision-making activities. The information architecture can provide a way to collect information from anywhere and make sense of it, delivering the support to wherever the decision maker is at the time.

Another barrier to the development of such a strategic information architecture is the business executive's seemingly insatiable desire for instant gratification. (Perhaps these executives have a great deal in common with toddlers!) The wonderful thing about the EIA is that it isn't a system—it is a set of standards that need to permeate everything, including spreadsheets, Web pages, existing decision support queries, and new operational systems. By putting the standard in place, even minor updates to existing resources make them instantly available through the searching tools that have been discussed in Chapter 8. Such an instant change can have an enormous "wow" factor when demonstrating how the portfolio of activities around a major customer can suddenly be made visible simply by asking the question in a search screen.

The tools used to access information across the organization need to be as consistent as the driving controls in different makes of car. While it is acceptable to have minor inconsistencies based on the job at hand and preferences of the main user groups, the basic operation and terminology of decision support systems should be consistent across all data sets and organizational divisions, just as in cars the accelerator and brake are always in the same relative positions.

The EIA needs to show everyone across the organization what information is where, how they can access it, and how they can directly help to improve access to that information for everyone. Making information available to everyone is not a task for a few specialists—it needs to be a task undertaken by everyone for the benefit of the whole enterprise.

NOTES

1. S. Heller, and E. Pettit (1998), *Design Dialogues* (New York: Allworth Press).
2. L. Rosenfeld and P. Morville (1998), *Information Architecture for the World Wide Web* (Sebastopol, CA: O'Reilly Media, Inc.)

Looking to the Future

An organization that understands the value of its information, and manages the asset accordingly, is equipped to deploy new products and services quickly, with a substantially reduced risk. The entire business case can be summed up by equating information management with business agility.

The last decade has seen rapid improvement in the success rates of information management technology projects (such as data warehouses and document management repositories) as practitioners have refined their solutions. Management still, however, struggles to understand the important role that information plays in their business. The winners of the future are going to be those businesses that understand this role and are among the first in their market to leverage it to its maximum potential.

This book has focused on the techniques needed to know what information exists, where it is, and how to get to it. With so much focus on having the right information to make decisions, it is surprising that the handling of data is still regarded as a technical mystery by the majority of executives.

While many readers will have found some of the ideas in this book technical, they will be second-nature to the next generation of business leaders. In the near future, information will be consistently valued as an economic asset with data moving within and across enterprise boundaries with commensurate changes being recorded on the balance sheets. Before this can happen, however, both technology and business have to change. Some of the technical constraints of data models and taxonomies need new and innovative solutions. Just as important, information management practitioners across all forms of structured and unstructured data have to agree on common approaches. The techniques of this book provide the linkage that the different disciplines need.

Similarly, business managers must accept that they are responsible for managing information just as they are responsible for managing business operations. It is no longer acceptable to assume that the information technology department is responsible for optimizing databases or document repositories. This book provides business leaders with metrics they can apply without needing to understand every detail of how the information is structured.

To this end, educators have a role to ensure that the discipline of Information Management is widely understood and that formal techniques to manage this most valuable resource are taught as part of both specialist and generalist courses.

Ultimately, everyone who handles information, regardless of its form, will want to know its relation to every other piece of information within and across enterprise boundaries. While consumers are, today, largely comfortable with providing their data within Web pages, in the future they will expect integration between business, government, and other parties with which they deal. To do this, systems are going to be needed with much more dynamic models and the ability to treat the data as part of the interface rather than as if they are somehow separate.

To illustrate how important this can be, consider the following diagram. Many types of organizations worry about their level of customer satisfaction. Generally, the customers with the simplest business interaction (such as just one product) are easy to satisfy by good staff service training. The customers who are most complex are usually so valuable that it is easy to justify investing in a highly personalized level of service. It is the middle group who are often left dissatisfied; their interactions are complex but not valuable enough to justify individualized attention. This middle group can be very profitable, as they often don't have the discount expectations of the high-value customers and are prepared to self-service if given the opportunity.

Customer Satisfaction to Complexity

Structuring information about their complex relationships, including all of the points that they interact with the organization, allows greater automation and proactive service processes to be introduced. This middle group is territory that has often been left by competitors who haven't invested in understanding the value they could provide.

Faced with making an investment in any aspect of a business operation, executives need to ask themselves how that investment improves the information asset. After all, this book has argued consistently that the value of most businesses is tied up in their information rather than their plant and equipment. Without the techniques that this book introduces, a business leader can only guess at the quantity and usability of the information being generated by a new investment. Armed with the metrics introduced here, they can quantify the information and its application. Such an approach allows for more rational decisions to be made.

An understanding of how to measure, structure, and transform around information will also allow businesses to innovate by designing products that maximize information, and hence value, for their stakeholders. The telecommunications carrier of the future can only differentiate by offering something useful beyond bandwidth to the consumer. The retailer of the future can only attract premium customers if they can inform those consumers in a way that is unique. The bank of the future will need to package together many services based on information that builds over the life of the customer relationship.

Readers of this book should now have an appreciation that information is a resource that needs to be actively planned, architected, and managed. The business that handles its information in such a way is able to become information driven. The information-driven business is agile, people-centric, and rich in the intellectual property that epitomizes successful enterprises in the twenty-first-century information economy.

About the Author

Robert Hillard was an original founder of MIKE2.0 (www.openmethodology. org), which provides a standard approach for information and data management projects. He has held international consulting leadership roles and provided advice to government and private sector clients around the world. He is a partner with Deloitte in Australia with more than twenty years' experience in the discipline, focusing on standardized approaches to information management including being one of the first to use XBRL in government regulation and the promotion of information as a business asset rather than a technology problem. Find out more at www.infodrivenbusiness.com.

Index

accounting, 1, 10, 156
 bodies, 21
agility, business, 28, 29, 65
algorithms, 2, 12, 46, 67, 71, 101, 172,
  186, 187, 188, 195
 cipher, 168, 170
 compression, 70
 data as, 116–118
 public key cryptography, 173
algorithms, text mining, 181
alternative hypothesis, 193
American Scientist, 105
annual report, 19, 99
anonymous matching, 173
AOL, 94
archiving of data, 132
Armstrong, Neil, 104
ARPANET, 5
ASCII, 87, 99–100
attributes
 audit change of, 133
 data quality, 165
 master data, 154
 metadata, 85, 87
 searching of, 96
attributes, stakeholder, 13, 38–40, 42, 46,
  53, 80, 138, 177, 179
time stamp, 49
audit subcommittee, 24, 27
audit trail, 133, 145

banks, 5, 20, 21, 58, 61, 65, 97, 150, 172,
  182, 196, 207
Bayes, Thomas, 187
Bayesian Probabilities, 187–191
beer distribution game, 117, 192–193
Berners-Lee, Tim, 94
bit
 computer, 3, 67, 69, 72
 information entropy defined, 68–70
Blair, Tony, 1
Blecher, Peter, 4, 108

blogs and blogging, 181, 183
Boltzmann's constant, 68
Boyce-Codd Normal Form (BCNF), 40,
  46
Building the Data Warehouse, The, 121
bullwhip effect, 192
business activity monitoring, 195–196
business applications, 37, 81, 89, 85–96,
  99, 121
business data, 4–5, 15
business history, 5
business intelligence, 121
business models, 5–6
business process, *See* Processes
business process outsourcing, 1
business process re-engineering, 30, 118
business rules, 49, 51, 112, 114–116, 120,
  172
 data quality, 160–162
 data retention, 132
 master data, 151

Cailliau, Robert, 94
call center, 97
candidate key, 39
cardinality, 38, 39–40, 44, 53, 106
CERN, 94
chaos
 taming, 119
 theory, 4, 103–120, 192
charter
 governance, 23–24, 26, 29, 31
 third-party data, 174, 182–183
chief data officer (CDO), 11, 24, 26, 29,
  31, 199
chief executive officer (CEO), 26, 164
chief financial officer (CFO), 27, 164
chief information officer (CIO), 11, 55, 90,
  199, 203
cipher, 168
 substitution, 168
Codd, Edgar F., 13, 37, 51, 79, 81, 123